GREAT ESCAPES

New Designs for Home Theaters by Theo Kalomirakis

This book was made possible with
the generous support of

RUNCO INTERNATIONAL
CURTCO ROBB MEDIA
CALIFORNIA AUDIO TECHNOLOGY (CAT)
MONACO AUDIO
XPLORE SOLUTIONS
IRWIN SEATING

To Jeanie Blum, Steve Tsubota, George Covas, Dan Kelleher, Nick Vernicos, Ed Kinsey, Tom Shoquist, and Jacques Schneider, who believed in me, gave me their friendship, and encouraged me to pursue dreams that are always alive and full of potential. This book is dedicated to them.

- Theo Kalomirakis

Library of congress Catalog Card Number: 2003109114

ISBN 0–8109–4634–3

Copyright © 2003 Theo Kalomirakis Theaters, Inc.

Photographs © 2003 Phillip Ennis

Published in 2003 by Harry N. Abrams, Incorporated, New York

Harry N. Abrams, Inc.

100 Fifth Avenue

New York, N.Y. 10011

www.abramsbooks.com

Abrams is a subsidiary of:

10 9 8 7 6 5 4 3 2 1

Printed and Bound in Greece by

KAPON EDITIONS

23-27 Makriyanni St., Athens GR - 117 42, Greece

e-mail:kapon_ed@otenet.gr

GREAT ESCAPES

NEW DESIGNS FOR HOME THEATERS BY THEO KALOMIRAKIS

BY STEVEN CASTLE

PHOTOGRAPHY BY PHILLIP ENNIS

WITH AN INTRODUCTION BY DEAN KOONTZ

HARRY N. ABRAMS, INC., PUBLISHERS

ACKNOWLEDGMENTS

"With a cast of thousands!" bragged the old movie ads. Well, that's almost how it feels when I think about how many people it took to translate sets of architectural drawings into exciting, exotic worlds of escape. The success of the theaters in the book, some of which took years to complete, depends largely on the skills and professionalism of hundreds of gifted audio/video installers, contractors, electricians, craftsmen, artisans, painters, sculptors, and interior designers who worked hard to bring these architectural designs to roaring life. Without them, there would be no Ritz or Moonlight or Toledo. The theaters in the book would have remained a set of beautifully drawn, two-dimensional plans on paper.

I would like to express my gratitude to the talented team of current and previous architects at our New York office that helped me design and manage the projects in this book and many others: Geoffrey Taylor, Jorge Arias, Aline Rizk, Yujin Asai, Garry Griggs, Michael Brothers, Robert Fuller, Anna Paola Civardi, Angela Kravtchenko, Richard Lanning, Donna Mikrut, Michael Soriano, Alejandro Gonzalez, David Hutchinson, and George Krassas. I am also grateful to Anthony Cortez, whose creativity in 3-D visualization has helped both me and our clients to see the end result before a project is built.

A well-designed theater would mean nothing without a superbly installed audio and video system. Our work would be half-completed without the invaluable contribution of Robert Kaufman and his associates of Audio Command Systems; Robert Eitel of Robert's Home Audio & Video; Anthony Pavia of Lights...Camera...Action...; Murray Kunis of Future Home; Bob Dodge and Jose Perez of Talk of the Town; Jason Abramowitz and Steve

D'Addone of IntraHome Technologies; Jeff Hoover of Audio Advisors; Greg Margolis of HomeTronics; Mark Hoffenberg of AudioVisions; Tom Doherty; Tony Tangalos, Rich Bara, and their associates; Scott and Jennifer Ross of Atlanta Home Theater; Don Calley of Image, Sound & Control; Tom Wells of Integrated Media Systems; Bill Anderson of Genesis Audio & Video; and Yannis Roumpessis.

All of the theaters in this book and many others came about because of the hard work of James Theobald, our dedicated sales and marketing director, who bonds with our clients and lets them know they will be in good hands once the project begins.

I would also like to thank Barry Silverstein, my trusted legal counsel, and Kevin Hall, my business adviser. Both are dear friends who have consistently supported me with their advice and guidance and kept me out of trouble time and again.

My gratitude also goes to the sponsors of this book, Runco International, Xplore Solutions, California Audio Technology (CAT), Monaco Audio, Irwin Seating, and Curtco Robb Media. Their generosity made *Great Escapes* possible.

I would like to thank Jeff Rubin, who art-directed the book with incredible flair and attention to detail; Steven Castle, who captured the personality of the theaters and their owners so eloquently in his writing; and my old friends Rahil and Moses Kapon, who produced the book with a lot of love in Greece. I also owe a lot to Phillip Ennis, who captured on film the magic of all the theaters in this book. He and his assistants—Ian Londin, John Rooney, and Bill Combs—breathed life into these theaters and made them look even more enchanting and inviting than they are in real life.

Finally, they may not be part of my professional landscape, but the love and support of Jeanie Blum and John Thomsen in this country and my brother Dimitris in Greece have made life a lot easier. They are my trusted family.

Theo Kalomirakis

CONTENTS

FROM THE HEART
By Theo Kalomirakis

It has been six years since the publication of Private Theaters, our first book featuring projects that a team of talented architects and I designed. There have since been many more theaters, numerous awards, great new projects, as well as a not-so-successful attempt to market our designs as products. Along the way, I learned some valuable lessons that will influence both my designs and my business decisions for years to come.

If you asked me to explain our business, I would give you the obvious answer: we design theaters. But on a more personal level, I would describe myself as someone who identifies right away with the inner child of those who love movies, and as one who helps them transform their typical moviegoing routines into enchanting rituals—inside their homes.

The connective tissue with my clients is my own passion for movies. I grew up loving movies simply because my family in Greece did not own a television until I was too old to become hooked by it. I vividly recall being no more than six years old and begging my grandpa to read me the movie listings in the local paper. Downtown Athens, where I was born, had an enviable cluster of movie palaces. They may not have rivaled their ornate American counterparts, but for me the Palace on Voukourestiou Street, the Rex, the Atticon, the Apollo, and the Orpheum on Stadiou Street were not just shrines to the art of the movies, but a passport to exotic cultures and lifestyles that completely took possession of my childhood and colonized my subconscious forever.

Every time a client asks me to recapture the golden glow of the downtown movie palace from his or her youth, I envision myself sitting in the elegant auditorium of the Apollo, mesmerized by the splendor of *West Side Story*, or in a velvet-upholstered mezzanine box at the Palace being scared out of my wits by Hitchcock's *The Birds*. I still remember taking in not only what was on the big screen but all the surrounding architectural beauty, half-lit by the glow of the silver screen. Since those days, watching a movie has been indelibly

connected in my mind with what is around me while I am in the theater. I believe that most people who grew up watching movies in elaborately designed movie palaces somehow feel the same, even if they are not always aware of it. For them, as it is for me, going to the movies encompasses much more than taking a break from shopping at the mall to catch whatever is playing at the local 25-plex. The ritual of crossing under a dazzling marquee and moving past an outer lobby, across a grand foyer, up a marble staircase, through an orchestra promenade, into the main auditorium, down aisle A, B, C, D, or E, and finally into a plush seat is what is sorely missing now. That's why even on a much smaller scale, home theater has brought back pleasures that just fifteen years ago we thought were lost forever.

The most valuable lesson I have learned in these past six years is to know what you are good at and to keep practicing it. I turned a deaf ear to invitations to design whole houses, simply because I did not want to compete with colleagues who got to be good because they designed houses exclusively. I stayed focused and

happy with designing theaters because for me, designing a theater is not unlike designing a house—albeit on a smaller, more intense scale.

My single regret is that at some point I succumbed to the temptation of merchandising my work by duplicating our one-of-a-kind designs into cookie-cutter home theaters. Maybe I just wanted to take a break from reinventing the home theater with each new design opportunity. Or maybe I thought that because the market was full of average-looking cookie-cutter theaters, I could come up with better-looking cookie-cutter designs. It was not so easy. . . . What I learned from this experiment was that you cannot migrate easily from being a service-oriented business to being a product manufacturer. My heart is invested in interacting directly with my clients. When six degrees of separation were introduced between my clients and me, that interaction was diluted and the magic was lost.

But nothing ventured, nothing gained, as they say. . . . This book amply demonstrates that there is nothing like a full-scale home theater, with its heart-stopping marquee, its lavish foyer, its mouthwatering concession stand, its inspiring auditorium. That's where my heart is—and for me, that's what a Great Escape is all about.

INTRODUCTION

By Dean Koontz

Theo Kalomirakis doesn't make the popcorn, but in creating any of his beautiful and dramatic home theaters, he does everything else. If he did provide the popcorn, he would need to research the subject of corn for three months, shop the world to locate the finest popping machine, commit himself to long hours of oil and salt analysis in a laboratory, and design a new and better popcorn tub or box. Theo is obsessed with his work and embarked upon a quest for an elusive ideal theater that can exist only in dreams. Each time that he makes a dream theater into a reality, no matter how stunning the creation, it never quite fulfills the ideal in his mind—and off he goes again in the enthusiastic pursuit of impossible perfection.

I understand this psychology all too well. The motivating certainty that your ideal is within your reach if only you can run a little faster and jump but one inch higher—this is the mighty engine that drives any committed novelist or painter or film director. This chase is crazy, of course, for it can never be won. Ours is a fallen world in which perfection can never be achieved. Besides, with the artist's every achievement, he further refines his ideal, makes it more enchanting, and thus it always remains the same few inches beyond his grasping fingers.

Nevertheless, in art and design, the pursuit of the ideal is as noble as it is sweetly foolish, and it gives us those moments of breathtaking beauty that lift our hearts out of darkness and strike in our minds bright fires of possibility. The ornate movie palaces of earlier eras—especially the Art Deco masterpieces like the Pantages Theater in Los Angeles—were more gorgeous and more inspiring than most of the films that played in them. They represent, after all, the clear vision of one architect and his close associates, while film is a medium that too often allows vision to be drowned in the rushing tide of expedient collaboration.

This irony informs the work of Theo Kalomirakis as well. His stunning home theaters, inspired by the magic of movies, have more magic, mystery, and grace than 98 percent of the films that will unspool in them. They are, therefore, not merely a joy to their owners but a service to the art of film, in the same sense that an exquisitely wrought Tiffany setting can make even a mediocre diamond shine like a crown jewel.

This book is eye candy to sweeten your mood on a sour day; however, it also gives you the opportunity to run with Theo Kalomirakis as he chases the ideal in his dreams, to feel the excitement of spinning magical

environments out of the golden threads of creative thought, and to recapture the wonder of going to the movies before theaters were reduced to drab multiplex boxes in which even that rare film of transcendent beauty is diminished by its setting. Theo is embarked not only on a quest for the ideal but on a crusade to redeem theater design, and it is always a thrill to take a ride with someone who, like him, has a glorious destination in mind and keeps the pedal to the metal.

BEHIND THE SCENES

THE COMPONENTS THAT
DELIVER GREAT PICTURE AND SOUND
FOLLOW A SCRIPT OF THEIR OWN

When you look at home theaters, particularly the ones that grace these pages, it is very easy to get caught up in the drama of the space, perhaps in how it recalls the ornate trimmings of the theaters from yesteryear, or reflects the contemporary lines of modern art, or even casts a creative eye to a fantastic future.

But none of these trimmings—none—would be possible without the technology that works behind the scenes to deliver great pictures and sound. Without these enablers, we don't enjoy the images that embrace beauty and challenge the imagination, and we don't experience sounds that place us in the middle of the action and provide a visceral, palpable sense to the power being witnessed on the screen.

Just as with the magic of the movies, these things are never as easy as they appear. On screen, the award-winning actor or actress delivers a brilliant line with grace, charm, and wit. But the audience typically never sees all the work that went into those few seconds, from the writers wrestling with dialogue to the actors rehearsing, to the player standing on his or her mark and delivering the line repeatedly until the perfect emotional impact is achieved. Meanwhile, all the workers behind the scenes are positioning the microphones and manning the cameras and preparing the actors with the proper amounts of makeup and hairspray and confidence to create this illusion.

Home theater technology certainly shines brightly today: This small arc-lamp assembly (right) from video projector manufacturer Runco International contains a quarter-size 700-watt Xenon lamp that can illuminate a 30-foot-wide screen.

Fast-forward to a DVD of this production brought home and ready for your enjoyment. To experience the full effect of that singular line, a different sort of production occurs. The cameraman is replaced by a video display, the microphone operators by an array of speakers and amplifiers and other electronics, the director by sophisticated processors that issue the commands for lights, camera, and action electronically. It's a precision ballet of signals that enact the perfect timing and tone and timbre—if well done—to bring you that one brilliant line, just as the film director intended.

Now multiply this dance thousands of times over, and you have the making of a movie enjoyed in a true home theater. The technological players behind a good home theater, it could be said, follow a script of their own. . . .

The scene here is a home theater, be it one that shimmers in the fanciful designs or one that is modestly appointed, with comfortable seating for family and friends.

The players are an ensemble of audio and video equipment, from the video projector or monitor to the loudspeakers and amplifiers to audio/video processors and control systems that can even dim the lights on cue.

The story line is that the audio and video equipment must work together with perfect timing and grace to deliver the sights and sounds of a film, just as the director intended them to be experienced.

The action begins at a remote control. A button is pressed, and . . .

(The lights dim.)

In addition, the DVD player cues up, the audio/video processor and amplifiers come on, the video projector bulbs light, and perhaps a fanfare trumpets.

The opening scene deftly transports the audience to a fantasyland, the stunning visuals painting a clear new world of untold promise, while the audio provides the sonic cues that secure their suspension of disbelief.

Behind the scenes, though, the potential for conflict reigns as dark as any great film noir. The many design elements in a theater room can conspire to compromise the performance of the audio and video. Columns and other decor can be in the way of optimum speaker placement. Hard surfaces of wood and glass can reflect sound too harshly. Bright colors can reflect back onto the screen, coloring the picture.

The decor of a home-theater room can certainly set the stage and tone for your great escape into another world, even providing an instant transport to another place and time. But none of that matters when the lights go down. "The two most important elements to me are a big picture and big sound," says Theo Kalomirakis. "The design is only the wrapping paper around the technology."

That doesn't mean you have to be a technophile to enjoy great home theater, because the end result is what you see and hear and whether you enjoy it. That's the bottom line.

Just ask Sam Runco, owner of video-projector manufacturer Runco International, who talks about fighting for years over the placement of his projectors— whether they should be placed on the floor or hung from the ceiling. Then he realized something. "The radio once had a place in the room, the TV was centered in a certain place in the room, but it's about where the projector actually shows, and that's the picture on the screen," Runco says.

The choices available today in video are astounding. You can have expensive, cathode-ray-tube (CRT) projectors that can show filmlike images, or the latest in video-projection technology, Digital Light Processing (DLP) projectors that display vivid and bright images. Other digital-projection technologies are emerging as well.

Smaller rooms can have still have large screens with a wide array of rear-projection TVs, flat-panel plasma monitors that can hang on the wall and are only a few inches thick, and conventional TVs. In any case, the advent of high-definition television (HDTV) will make these images so crisp and clear, you'll swear they are real.

The audio portion of the home theater has undergone a similar revolution in the last decade, progressing from a TV or other video display *possibly* being connected to a pair of stereo speakers, to an array of speakers that provide true surround sound so you will be immersed in a movie by hearing all of the sounds around you, just as you do in real life.

In a good surround-sound system, you will not only hear and feel special effects such as explosions and rumbles, you will also clearly hear the softest dialogue as if coming from the actors' lips, sense crickets chirping around you during night scenes, or hear a car or plane pass by and fade away realistically.

You can have these speaker arrays in what is referred to as 5.1 (five full channels and a subwoofer just for low bass sounds) or 7.1 (seven channels and a subwoofer)—perhaps even as many as ten main channels and thirty subwoofers. And with the emergence of multichannel audio that uses several channels to record and play back audio on DVD-Audio (DVD-A) and Super Audio CD (SACD) discs, you could enjoy an immersive concert experience right in your home.

"The audio quality in your home can actually surpass that in reality," says Brian Barr, president and CEO of custom-loudspeaker manufacturer California Audio Technology (CAT). "People are enjoying video jazz concerts and symphonies right in their homes, and you can hear the detail of all the instruments equally, whereas in a live jazz club or symphony, the instruments will sound louder or softer to you based on your position in the audience."

All these speakers in the home theater also need to be powered, and that's where amplification comes in. Amplifiers basically deliver the appropriate electrical juice for the speakers to pump out the sound. But there are differences between them. "A good amplifier can maintain power during a period of peak demand, when there's a lot of action a going on in the movie or musical performance," says Greg Margolis, president of HomeTronics, a high-end custom-electronics contractor and cofounder of Monaco Audio amplifiers. "And during quiet scenes they should run quiet, without any background noise or distortion."

In many cases, none of this audio wizardry would work without acoustical balance. Placing the proper amounts of reflective sound material in some areas and diffusive or absorptive materials in others can smooth out any sonic trouble spots in a room and give it a balanced, more natural sound, advises acoustician Steven Haas, principal of SH! Acoustics.

Last but certainly not least, control systems can be vital to operating all these different audio and video components without having to use several remotes. There's a revolution taking place here as well, and it's called IP (for Internet Protocol) control, which basically allows you the ease of operating your home theater or the electronics throughout your house as if you are surfing through World Wide Web pages—and without waiting for timely downloads.

Control systems today give people so many more options. "You can have what you want, when you want it, and how you want it," says Dan Kippycash, CEO of Xplore Solutions, a web-based control-systems company.

Now here's our big end-of-the-script twist: technologies such as web-based control in the home, DLP projectors, and surround-sound audio are making home-theater systems much more affordable and accessible for everyone.

After all, the home theater never would have been possible without the popularity of VCRs in the 1980s and videotapes made available to people to watch movies in their homes, so we all could get a sense of Hollywood at home, just like the film moguls with their elaborate screening rooms.

"It's going to reach critical mass now, especially as people build homes and put home theaters in as part of their mortgages, because it's so easy to do," says Sam Runco. "And anything that drives new homes will also drive interest for home-theater retrofits."

And that's good for everyone. Our little home-theater script comes to a happy ending after all. All the technical elements have worked in harmony to provide an enjoyable experience. In reality, though, this ending is but a beginning to bringing the enjoyment and escape of a home theater to everyone.

This acoustic engineering diagram from California Audio Technology (CAT) shows how an array of correctly placed loudspeaker drivers can provide accurate and even sound to all listening positions.

THEATERS
OF
DREAMS

THEATERS OF DREAMS

OVERTURE TO THEATERS

A great home theater is much more than a place to watch movies or view concerts. It is much more than a collection of parts that immerse us in lifelike images and sounds. This is what Theo Kalomirakis provides. A step inside one his theaters produces an instant transport to another place or time—and all the drama that should accompany the viewing of a great movie.

Moreover, each theater is a unique personal statement, reflecting the values, ideals, and dreams of the people behind them. One theater recalls the grandeur of an era long gone and the infinite possibilities that existed, while another harks back to gentler times in turn-of-the-century England, and yet another revisits the refined glamour once called Hollywood.

A theater owner in Las Vegas chooses to travel back to the riches of an ancient culture, while a Georgia couple is transported to the Italian countryside, and a California family honors the Moorish style. A retired baseball star enjoys a timeless venue, while another former baseball star savors Miami Beach sunsets a continent away.

One theater houses great works of art, and another is, in effect, a work of modern art.

Moreover, these theaters represent quality time, such as the futuristic one enjoyed by an entire extended family. Another contemporary theater brings a far-flung family closer together. And the construction of still another theater inspired a couple to realize they had their own large and caring family working right in their home.

These theaters are time capsules, time machines, quality-time capsules and machines—and, ultimately, the canvases for their patrons to express their own wonderfully vivid dreams and ideals. And that is what makes them fantastic.

THE KIEV
THE GLORY OF OLD RUSSIA
IS RESTORED IN OPERATIC STYLE

With a mere step into its theater lobby, guests at this Ukrainian dacha sense they are about to experience something special. Rich tones of ruby, marble, and sky greet the eyes. The ceiling rises beyond the entry arch with panels of gold leaf seemingly set against portals to a cloudless expanse. Bold burgundies swirl gracefully in the lobby's center dome, and chandeliers dangle in forms of wistful petals. Portraits of movie idols Jean Harlow and Greta Garbo beckon guests to an opening framed with columns that glimmer with gold.

In an instant, it is all left behind, for words alone cannot describe what comes next. The entry is to a palace, to another time of grand and graceful opulence, a celebration of man's accomplishments and civility, of his artisanship and creativity, of prosperity and promise and his ever pressing forward toward new and exciting possibilities.

Like any palace guest, one can't help but gaze skyward here—to the bounty of flora in the heavenly dome. A harvest of gold reigns in the ceiling medallions, the silk-draped panels, the concave coffered ceiling beyond, and the regal proscenium arch trimmed in backlit gilt.

There's no doubt about it:
you are about to enter a very special place—
one of elegance, grandeur,
and the promise of infinite possibilities.

The ornate capitals in the lobby
may as well come from a St. Petersburg palace, displaying the will to extend
beyond the traditional and create the superlative.

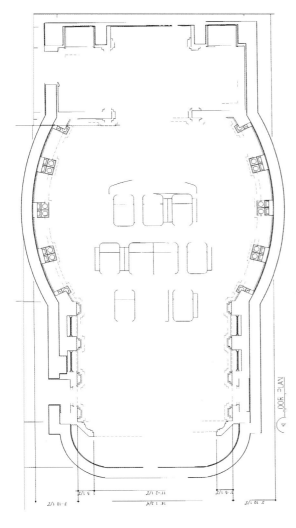

Along the walls, Ionic columns stand sentinel to more arches and silk panels and judiciously placed medallions, all crowned with rows of dentils. In the center hangs the unifying touch of a bronze-and-crystal chandelier. At once its candlesticks flicker skyward and its glass drips reflections to the more earthbound, defining in its branches all the richness and grace of this space. Perhaps, it could be said, reflecting that will in us all to savor such beauty.

And like a palace, this space is the offspring of both stately power and whimsical imagination. "I wanted to create an allegory of wishful thinking, that all of this existed before," says the theater's former owner, Dan Mysko, who renovated his entire dacha in the ever-optimistic and grand Belle Epoque style reminiscent of the palaces of St. Petersburg.

Local artisans assisted with the designs of ceiling and wall details, offering suggestions on how to best depict local flora in the elaborate swirls (right).

Mysko, a Ukrainian by birth but now a resident of Aspen, Colorado, directed the extensive renovations while serving as an adviser to the Ukrainian president during the post-Soviet 1990s. It was a new era, a forward-looking era of hope imbued with the promise of prosperity.

The drab-styled dacha had been a retreat for former Soviet leaders dating back to Joseph Stalin. In fact,

Intricacies delight throughout, from the fine lines of the hand-painted lobby dome (left) to the elegance of the chandelier, curtain fringes, and elaborate ceiling details.

a projection booth and 35mm projector, presumably for viewing propaganda films, were found in what is now the living room. Mysko had the space of the theater added, clad in concrete, and had plans, he says, to install a "plain old theater."

Those plans changed with the available pool of affordable local labor. In all, a small economy of local artisans, from sculptors to painters, worked on the dacha and its theater, custom-crafting the moldings and capitals and other architectural details, painting the decorative flora on the ceilings and walls, applying the gold leaf, even offering design suggestions to achieve the proper representation of local flavor and style. The costs of building such a theater elsewhere would have been prohibitive.

Several challenges confronted the designers in creating a theater in the space. For one, the rounded walls and dome created an echo that had to be treated acoustically. The solution was to create a sub-dome—a dome within a dome—a couple of feet beneath the concrete structure and to fill the void with materials to eliminate the echo. Some of the fabrics, such as the Indian silk used in the ceiling panels, could not be purchased locally, so they were bought in places such as New York and shipped overseas. Even the design for the decorative capitals on the lobby columns was inspired by those in New York's Shubert Theater. In all, the project took four years, because everyone involved, from the designers to the artisans, wanted it to be right. They knew they were working on something that was special.

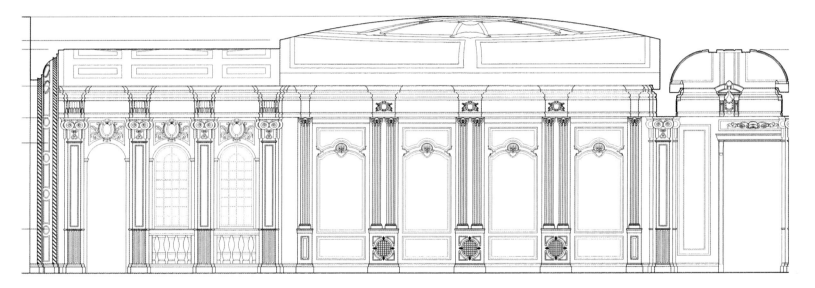

Although he had occasional guests, Mysko wanted the theater mostly for himself. "At that time, there wasn't much to do here," he says. "And I am a fan of classic movies."

He also has a fine appreciation for classic movie theaters. "My favorite part of this theater is how very impressive it is when you walk into it, and the richness of it all," he says. "For me, personally, the theater is a fantasy. It is an escape, like the theaters of old were an elaborate escape for people."

Mysko's escape into fantasy involved some additional drama. The gold medallions in the ceiling conceal lights that illuminate the dome, and as the house lights dim the 20th Century-Fox theme plays to trumpet the start of the movie.

The medallions between the panel sections shine spotlights on the ceiling, very nearly casting a spell on visitors.

His most memorable moment in this theater palace, though, was viewing the timeless *Casablanca* on the 130-inch-wide screen. "It made me feel like I was watching it in an old movie theater," Mysko recalls. It seems almost fitting that such a theater would screen an enduring romance set in a foreign land, as world politics intermingle with enterprise and hope and the personal trials of both to evoke a lasting portrait of the human spirit. And a pretty good story as well.

Fantasy? Perhaps, like those grandiose palaces made to conjure feelings of Oz-like awe, but fantasy resides only upon the surface of this palatial theater. It is all about possibilities and the wonderful accomplishments that can result.

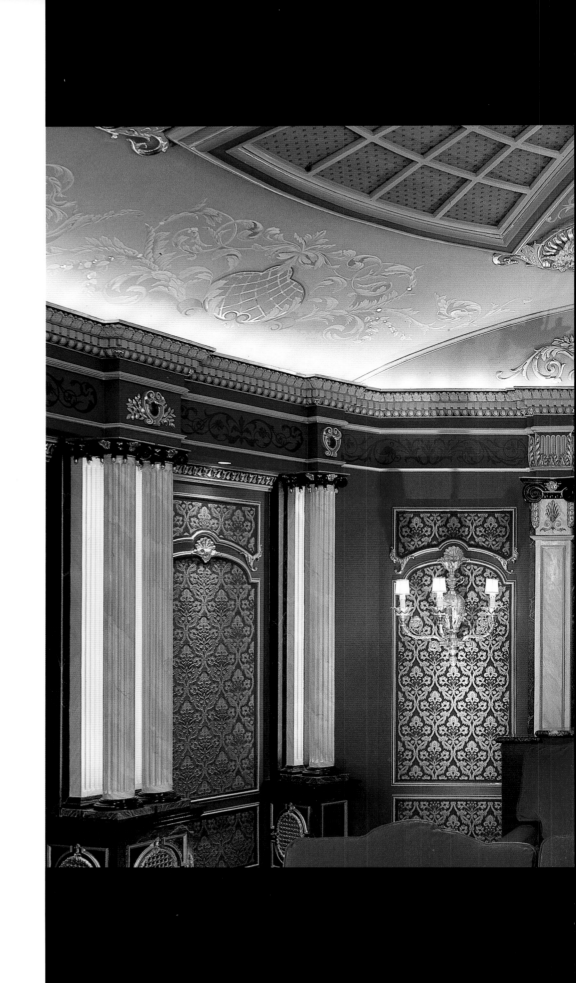

Beneath the lovely dome, guests can sink into the plush seating, focus their attention on the screen,

and be transported to new and exciting possibilities.

THE ELLIPSE

A lot of effort goes into keeping a family together. There's the fostering of open communication, the building of trust, the nurturing of togetherness. And for Mark Iola, there was also the construction of a high-tech home theater.

"We were looking for something for our house that gives our whole family a sense of community," says Iola, who has three boys ages five through sixteen and two brothers who live nearby with children of their own. In all, the Iola clan boasts seven children ages five through eight and fifteen through eighteen, all of whom share rights to this entertaining space. "The younger kids will watch movies like *Monsters, Inc.* and *Ice Age* early in the evening; then the teenagers watch their movies later."

At first glance, you may not think such a high-tech theater was built as an extended family entertainment space. Enter and you might think you were on the starship *Enterprise*. The room is elliptical in shape, with a huge lighted oval in the ceiling soffit bearing a sunburst in relief. Ahead, a brightly lit proscenium of square panels beckons like something from *Close Encounters of the Third Kind.*

Call this Close Encounters of the Family Kind, with high technology in mind. In the modest-sized space are fourteen seats as well as four barstools in the back, though the Iolas once sat twenty-six preschoolers for a class outing, with the kids sharing seats.

The stainless-steel marquee only hints at the technological wonders to be found inside.

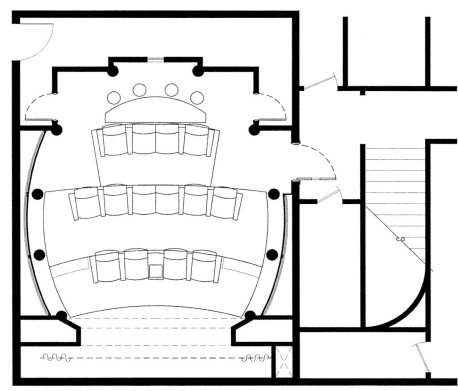

The Iolas had seen another of Theo Kalomirakis's round theater designs and liked the look of it. They also wanted superior sound quality, which is difficult to accomplish in a circular space. "Theo designed everything in this theater with acoustics in mind," says Iola. That meant fabric walls were used between the columns, and some significant treatments were put in place to absorb and reflect sound in all the right places and prevent any noise from escaping into other parts of the house.

The theater has many more high-tech amenities, including a commercial-grade Digital Light Processing (DLP) projector, the latest in home-theater projection technologies, and customized speakers in the side walls to throw just the right amount of sound to the front and back of the room. A subwoofer beneath the floor in the back shakes the seats during action sequences. There's also a connection to hook up a laptop computer, to preview PowerPoint presentations, and two DVD players for convenience when switching from one disc to another. In addition, the entire room was made wheelchair-accessible for one of the family's friends.

The proscenium framing the screen is made up of stainless-steel mesh and acrylic panels backlit for a high-tech effect.

Even the construction of the room was high-tech, requiring that each wall and ceiling panel be manufactured with laser-guided instruments. Then the two curved sides of the theater were fitted together within a tiny degree of tolerance.

The result, says Iola, is "a special place, where everything in the real world goes away."

Except for family and friends, that is. The Iolas even combined their DVDs into one library of about 1,000, stored in the back of the room and organized by category in a book and computerized database. "We're the Blockbuster of our family, with people signing out videos all the time," says Iola.

And that's all right with this family man. "We wanted it so when friends and family come over they can fire it up," Iola says. "It's been really great for keeping everyone together. I can spend time with all my family under my roof, and it's good for me as a dad because I can watch over the kids a lot better in my own house."

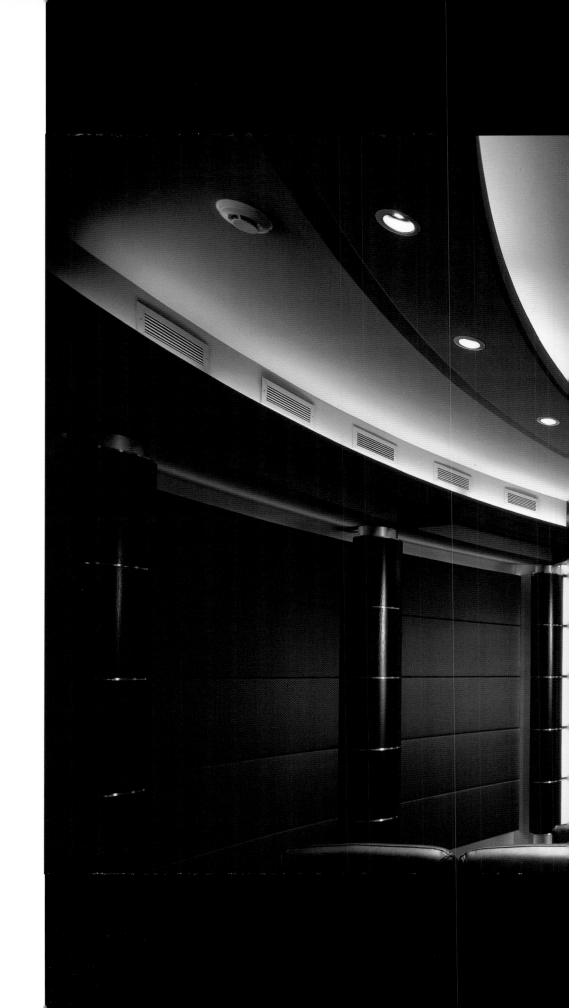

The ceiling's silver-leaf starburst provides some visual excitement, and the oval shape of the room required carefully calculated acoustics.

THE MOONLIGHT
An Architectural Masterpiece for
a Best-Selling Author and His Wife

An editor once told best-selling author Dean Koontz that on the deepest level, all his suspense novels were about the same thing: wounded people unexpectedly forming a family as they come together in a fight against adversity. Through widely different story lines, Koontz's many characters come to realize and appreciate the bonds formed when relying on others—and the individual strength derived from their mutual caring.

"They're all on a quest for a family and a home," says Koontz, though he may as well be speaking of his own long journey. He and his wife, Gerda, have scratched their way from a hardscrabble beginning to their new and luxurious sanctuary overlooking the Pacific. Dean's childhood in particular was fueled by desperation and violence.

"It's tremendously humbling," Koontz explains. "Gerda and I were married with 150 bucks and a used car, so it's amazing to walk through our new

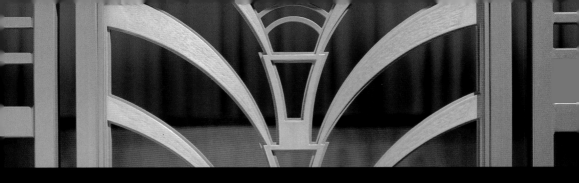

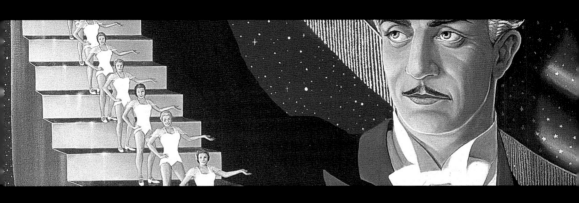

A chorus line of Art Deco details dance throughout this elaborate production,
from the bronze railings to the movie posters to the Michael Graves designed sconces on the façade.

home and see the way the unique Southern California light comes through the windows, and to find exquisite sculpture in the architecture at every turn."

The house, ten years in the making, blends into two and a half acres in the low-slung architectural style of Frank Lloyd Wright, complete with the use of natural materials and a flow of spaces remaining true to human scale, all the while revealing wondrous surprises in the spirit of Wright's architecture.

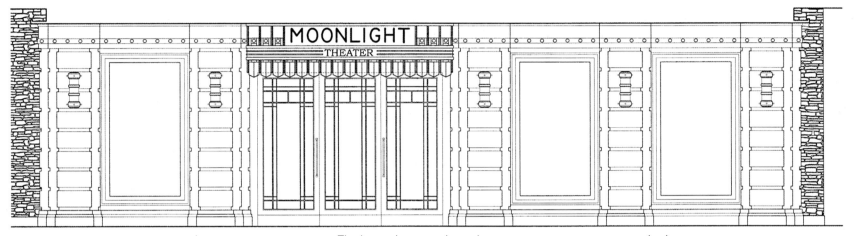

The home theater and its adjoining spaces are no exception. In designing it, Theo Kalomirakis used cues from Wright's famous Unity Temple in Oak Park, Illinois, so the theater is entered through a series of right turns: through the front doors from a hallway of stacked stone, by a box office that opens to a larger lounge area, and to the theater itself, an expansive inner sanctum lit by stained-glass "skylights" and ringed by balconies

designed to give everyone who gathers there a full and equal view. The theater somehow projects the same sort of reverence for community as does Wright's famous temple. Ample light shines from above, and the audience is granted as dignified a position as the proscenium. It's a very democratic space.

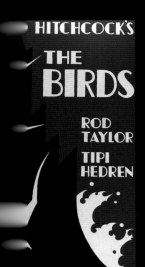

HITCHCOCK'S
THE
BIRDS

ROD
TAYLOR
TIPI
HEDREN

THE THIN MAN

KING KONG

THE 7 GREAT ZIEGFELD

BOGART
THE BIG SLEEP

You won't find these movie posters elsewhere.

From the box office to the lounge, no details were missed,

not in the bronze and mica capitals, the Wrightian sculpture on the bar,

or the mural above with its Deco race and cityscape.

Like that famous architect, the Koontzes are obsessed with detail. As a writer, Dean fears receiving letters from readers challenging details in his books, so he conducts meticulous research on all his subject matter. That same attention to detail went into overseeing the design and construction of the home and its sizable home-theater space.

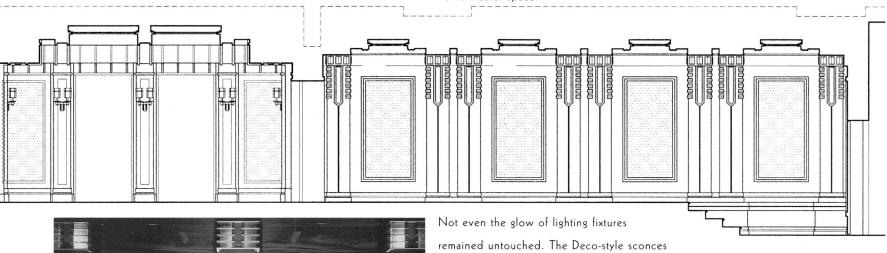

Take your Top Hat off to these movie posters.
Fred and Ginger—and Errol Flynn—would be proud.

Not even the glow of lighting fixtures remained untouched. The Deco-style sconces outside the entrance to the theater, though designed by renowned architect Michael Graves, received a layer of shellac to produce a more golden light. Inside, the bronze and mica backlit capitals crowning the columns received numerous coats of shellac to soften the light from harsh fluorescent bulbs, which had to be used because of the limited space within the columns.

Even the numerous posters didn't escape the Koontzes' discerning eyes. "We wanted to have posters of Art Deco—era movies with Art Deco lettering and style, but we found that the posters for those movies were the typical garish movie posters," says Koontz. So the couple hired illustrator Phil Parks, who had illustrated some children's books with Dean, and Parks made posters of their Deco dreams.

Koontz also had an Art Deco book jacket of John O'Hara's novel *Appointment in Samarra*, so he had Parks design a poster for that as well, though no movie of the novel had ever been made. "I even cast the film and put Robert Mitchum and others in it. I figured no one would know there had never been a movie," says Koontz. "Then we had a party to open the house, and my film agent said, 'There was no movie of *Appointment in Samarra*.' I asked him how he knew, and he said he represented the estate of John O'Hara. I thought no one would notice that poster, but someone found me out in only one day!"

That's one more reason for Koontz to obsess with detail, such as in the stained-glass panels in the theater ceiling, through which the light is dispersed evenly by shining from four sides and onto all reflective surfaces behind the panels, providing uniform illumination in the Wright-inspired designs.

A Wrightian sculpture also enhances the face of the bar counter in the lounge area. Some materials originally to be used for the bar front included acrylic panels, but upon close inspection the Koontzes could see the seams. Other people might not notice, but Dean and Gerda would know, and that bothered them. "Compromise in art and architecture is the death of quality," Koontz says. "So we always use authentic materials."

The entrance to the theater blends into the rich woods of sapele and quilted maple, but the door's stained-glass window hints at what awaits.

The box office opens to a larger lounge, the ceiling displaying the first glimpse of the theater's motif.

The lounge area is sheathed in exotic woods such as sapele and quilted maple, highlighted by bronze and gold leafing, materials that were used during the Art

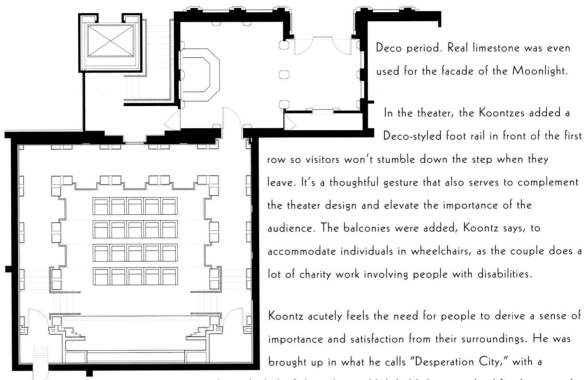

The theater opens to back and side hallways with several small balconies that frame the auditorium.

Deco period. Real limestone was even used for the facade of the Moonlight.

In the theater, the Koontzes added a Deco-styled foot rail in front of the first row so visitors won't stumble down the step when they leave. It's a thoughtful gesture that also serves to complement the theater design and elevate the importance of the audience. The balconies were added, Koontz says, to accommodate individuals in wheelchairs, as the couple does a lot of charity work involving people with disabilities.

Koontz acutely feels the need for people to derive a sense of importance and satisfaction from their surroundings. He was brought up in what he calls "Desperation City," with a violent, alcoholic father who couldn't hold down a job. After he married his high-school sweetheart, Gerda, and they moved to a poor coal-mining town, the Koontzes rented a house for fifty dollars a month—which they couldn't afford, but it was the only one for rent that had indoor plumbing. Dean had been brought up using an outhouse and wouldn't—couldn't—live like that again. He also needed a space that inspired him.

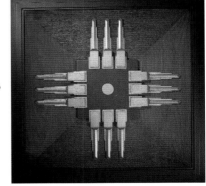

Nearly a continent away and a few decades later, Koontz has just that. "You need to bring yourself to a peaceful place to write," he says. "So this is my quest for the ultimate work space, and our lifelong campaign to have a beautiful space where we can feel safe."

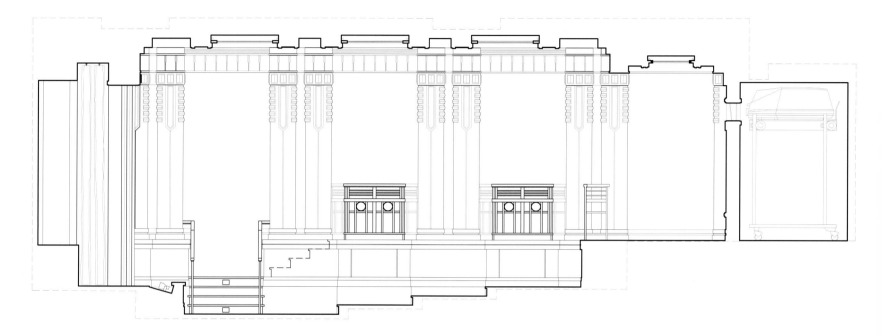

Bronze claddings on the columns provide a strong centering, while stained-glass coffers cast a warm light.

Koontz hasn't forgotten his humble beginnings. The theater is named the Moonlight after his and Gerda's hometown drive-in theater in Bedford, Pennsylvania. The community's more ornate, indoor theater was named the Pitt—but, well, Koontz isn't quite that humble.

Although their quest for a beautiful space took much of the last ten years, the Koontzes don't regret it. Dean and Gerda knew it would take several years of patient toil to do everything right. One thing they do regret is no longer being surrounded by the big family of friends who worked so long on their house. "When you meet craftsmen and tradesmen who have a passion for their work and an eye for detail—well, that's the same attitude of a writer or a fine painter," explains Koontz.

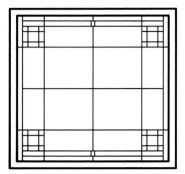

"So a lot of our friends of long duration are in the home-building trades, and we made even more friends through this process. For a long time, as we built this house, we could go there and always find this extended family. The completion of the project was, therefore, almost a disappointment."

It's as if the Koontzes and their friends are characters in one of Dean's books, coming together to form a family where everyone is important. And just as in his books, this story ends with our main characters, Dean and Gerda Koontz, finding their own family and home—at long last.

*The layout of the theater was
inspired by Frank Lloyd Wright's dignified Unity Temple.*

THE FIRST RUN

Baseball is an enduring game, not because of strong men mashing home runs or pitchers hurling fire, but because the game is played with a certain element of faith. It's an endlessly optimistic game, often dappled in sunshine and meandering in pace, slowly building in nuances of suspense, its dramatic flairs eventually rewarding the faithful. It's also a timeless event, absent a clock and played in ballparks that manage to provide escapes to a simpler time, while never compromising today's modern amenities.

In these ways, baseball is like watching a great movie in a great movie house. There's the sense of escape, the timeless feel of the venue, layers of plot that build and build. So it's no surprise that the baseball star who owns this home theater wanted a timeless venue for his own family's entertainment.

Entering this room is akin to absorbing that first glimpse of green as you ascend from a ballpark tunnel. In a short step or two, the entire field expands before you in delightful splendor. The simplest of combinations—the green of the grass, a diamond of earth, the outfield walls—form an authentically pleasing architecture.

Now replace the grass with a carpet of sage, the earth with columns of polished walnut, the sun's warming rays with a golden glow of light, the cement aisles with a promenade that circles the back in a promise of comfort and style, the hard-backed seats with overstuffed chairs—and you have this ageless home-theater venue.

The streamlined marquee and woods display a postmodern edge to what is a timeless design.

In baseball movie terms, this theater is a *Field of Dreams*, one that begins with the owner's wish for a home-entertainment space to match the contemporary decor in the family's home and built on the faith that it could be something special, its architects ever designing on that edge between success and something less. Start with the room's oval design: not a typical home-theater space, and one that is quite often problematic.

Kalomirakis brought in some timeless Art Deco elements to the contemporary design, in the form of the Deco-style panels of mica and metal and bronze near the front, the celestial chandelier of mica that the casts a golden glow on this venue, and the mica-covered lights above the rear promenade.

This theater-in-the-round contains all authentic materials, requiring no paint or faux finishes, from the polished walnut to the bronze capitals topping them to the fabric walls and custom-made chairs, creating a rich and natural texture.

The round shape of the room presented some challenges for the sound and video system, designed and installed by Tom Wells of Integrated Media

Polished-walnut paneling and the large mica light bathe the theater in a soft amber glow.
The side panels of bronze and mica add a Deco touch.

There is ample legroom and modern amenities,
including a touch-screen control built into the projector enclosure and

Systems. "In oval rooms, the sound tends to reflect and get focused in the front," he says. "So we applied a lot of acoustical absorption material in the back, where you would normally use materials that diffuse the sound."

Speakers for side and rear surround sound were installed within the walnut columns. For Wells, the theater, built several years ago, marked the first time his company had installed multiple speakers in the side and rear walls, though that is common today. It was unintentional, but the name of the theater became more than a double-entendre connoting baseball and the movies; it also marked the First Run for some innovations in home-theater electronics. "We really didn't know how it was going to sound," Wells recalls. "But it has a nice rich and warm sound."

The owners do have some high-tech amenities in this timeless venue. They can view video from the camera at the front of the house on the touch-panel control, and a light alerts them to any sounds emanating from the children's rooms at night, so they can check on the children. The owner also has a video-editing studio in a room nearby.

Modern amenities, a timeless design, and authentic materials provide these homeowners with a natural and ageless escape. And like a good baseball game or movie, it is textured with layers of subtle drama. It's an enduring theater for a player of an enduring game.

THE NILE

EGYPTIAN SPLENDOR
IN A DIFFERENT DESERT

Las Vegas is a world tour of tastes, with samples of Venice, Paris, and New York. And for those who want to be like an Egyptian, there's even a big black pyramid with motion-simulator rides. One thing many of these attractions lack, however, is a real sense of what it may be like in these exotic settings and times. It's hard to get beyond the kitsch and jingle-jangle of slot machines while swooning to cultural thrill rides.

Away from the Strip in an exclusive enclave is such a place, a very private place where world culture and history combine in a lavish setting. It's filled with both a seriousness of purpose and a sense of fantasy, in a setting tinged with the bittersweet.

And so, Joan Winchell found, was Egypt when she first visited it several years ago. A self-proclaimed Egyptologist, she has always had a fascination with the land and its culture. "I practically lived in the museums and the field. I got in the tombs and absorbed the beauty of everything," she says.

A golden sculpture of King Tutankhamen lords over this lavish interpretation of life in the Valley of the Nile.

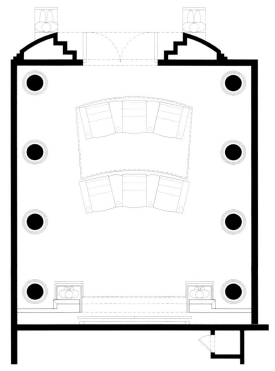

The mysteries of how the Egyptians built the pyramids and their alignment with celestial bodies still perplexes scholars today, but Winchell was interested in something more. "I tried to imagine what it was like to live in their rooms."

More than a decade later, when she and her husband, Verne, decided to have a home theater built in their Las Vegas home away from home, Egypt didn't immediately come to mind. All they knew was that as much as they loved the Art Deco design of their California home's theater, also designed by Theo Kalomirakis, they didn't want to repeat it. "Then my husband suggested we do something Egyptian," Winchell says.

The couple wanted to capture the feeling of being in an Egyptian room or temple, as well as immerse themselves and their guests in the ancient culture's richness. The experience begins at the door to the theater, with a door handle in the shape of a cobra with an eye of opal. The cobra was a symbol depicted both in Egyptian myths and in the headdresses of the pharaohs to protect them.

Painstakingly carved hieroglyphics adorn the cast-limestone proscenium and columns.

Inside is ancient Egypt, complete with the Valley of the Nile and the culture's mythology. Columns adorned with hieroglyphics frame colorful murals of the Nile on one side and the desert on the other, as a golden sculpture of King Tutankhamen stands in front of the cast-stone proscenium. Above are a series of outstretched griffon vulture wings, an Egyptian symbol also used on the ceilings of temples for protection. The red domes represent the sun and an Egyptian solar myth in which the creator and sun god, Ra, is bitten by a snake and must reveal his secret name in order for a healing spell to take effect. He agrees if he can reveal his secret name only to Horus, as represented by a falcon or vulture.

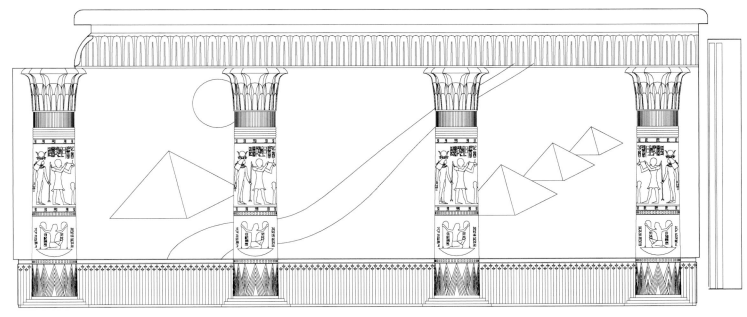

The bas-relief of the cast-bronze proscenium doors depicts an offering made to a ruler. Griffon vulture wings adorn not only the ceiling (previous spread), but the tops of the columns as well (left).

The vulture wings are repeated atop the reconstituted limestone columns, scale replicas of those from Egypt's famous Temple of Amun, so it appears that you are looking out at the Nile from between the columns.

A little like the incredible labor that went into constructing the pyramids, some dedicated work went into the detailing of this theater. Sculptor Frank Gallagher worked full-time for two and a half years carving the hieroglyphics by hand. "Verne and Joan are patrons of the arts. They gave me the ability to do some innovative work," says Gallagher.

Like the works of the ancients, some mysteries remain in this theater. Gallagher says he spent nine months devising a process to create the proscenium doors' bonded bronze bas-relief of figures making an offering to their ruler. However, he won't reveal the secrets of his process.

Joan Winchell is proud of her Egyptian theater. She says the feeling her visitors have is similar to her own feeling of awe when touring Egypt. "They can't believe the workmanship in it. They touch things and feel things," she says, as if they have to see if it's real. But she also can't help but be reminded of her husband, Verne, who passed away a few months before the theater was completed. "I'm happy about the theater, but I'm also sad," she says. "I see this as a monument to him."

This monument to Verne Winchell, it turns out, also pays homage to an entire culture of monuments.

Looking out to the mural of the Nile from the columns

provides the sense of being in an Egyptian temple in another time.

THE JEWEL
ARTFULLY ACHIEVED HARMONY IN
COASTAL FLORIDA

As the owner of a modern-style house, Larry DeGeorge had only a couple of criteria for his home theater. "It had to be contemporary looking and easy on the eyes," he says. In other words, DeGeorge wanted a pleasing balance of form, color, and texture in his modern theater. What he enjoys today is all that, in a room that is itself a piece of modern art.

This home theater unfolds in layers of meaning, revealing in its surfaces, colors, and form something that is not merely what it appears to be, but so much more.

One enters a hall that partially reveals the theater room between polished mahogany columns. The first glimpse over the granite-topped footwalls only hints at how the soothing earth tones blend with neat linear forms. Black lines bisect the top of a column. A light box of intersecting lines forming squares and rectangles appears in the frieze between two other columns.

Turn the corner into the room, and the focal point is the light-box frieze of lines and shapes nearly encircling the sitting area. Angled mahogany panels decorate a portion of the back wall. Above is a large ceiling structure that conceals the projector, and above that, a multilevel soffit.

Step back, and there's a proscenium of light and hint of the light box above, placed off-center. Even the apron of the stage angles subtly.

To enter the Jewel is to step into a piece of modern art, this a canvas of mahogany, mica, and luxurious fabrics.

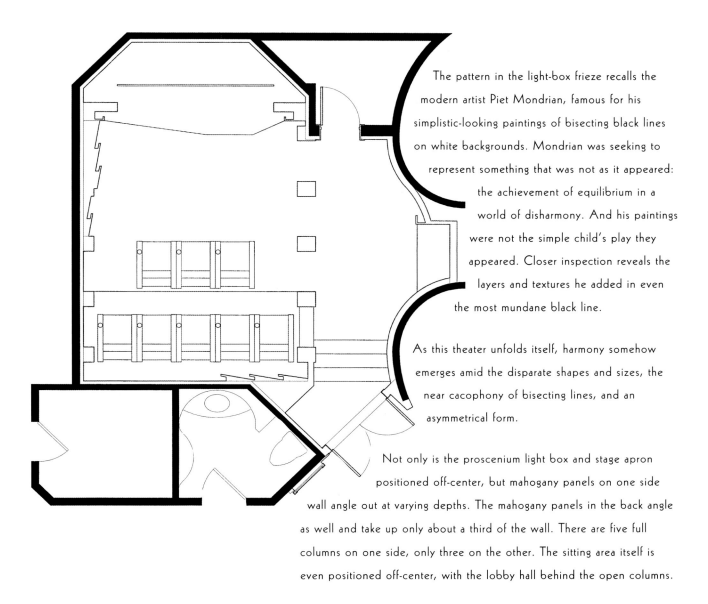

The pattern in the light-box frieze recalls the modern artist Piet Mondrian, famous for his simplistic-looking paintings of bisecting black lines on white backgrounds. Mondrian was seeking to represent something that was not as it appeared: the achievement of equilibrium in a world of disharmony. And his paintings were not the simple child's play they appeared. Closer inspection reveals the layers and textures he added in even the most mundane black line.

As this theater unfolds itself, harmony somehow emerges amid the disparate shapes and sizes, the near cacophony of bisecting lines, and an asymmetrical form.

Not only is the proscenium light box and stage apron positioned off-center, but mahogany panels on one side wall angle out at varying depths. The mahogany panels in the back angle as well and take up only about a third of the wall. There are five full columns on one side, only three on the other. The sitting area itself is even positioned off-center, with the lobby hall behind the open columns.

The theater's lobby is a side hallway separated by a granite-topped footwall. Difficult design elements, such as the curved walls behind a grand staircase, were resolved by situating the sitting space off-center.

But just when one thinks it's all off-kilter, symmetry emerges. The missing columns on the left reveal themselves at the top. Black-lined capitals grace the tops of the facing columns in the rear. Even the seemingly random lines of two facing light boxes are mirror images. A certain balance emerges from the disparate elements. Harmony conquers disharmony. What appears to be on the surface isn't quite.

The finish materials help to create a whole more harmonious than the sum of its parts. The light boxes are made from mica, backlit to exude a soft,

rice-paper effect. The rich, polished mahogany of the columns and wall panels perfectly frame the soothing tones of the chairs, carpets, and stage curtain.

The greatest challenge in achieving this harmony was creating a balanced sound as well. A concrete casing, two curved walls behind a grand staircase, and a seventeen-foot-high ceiling made the space acoustically challenging, to say the least. The curved walls were partially concealed in

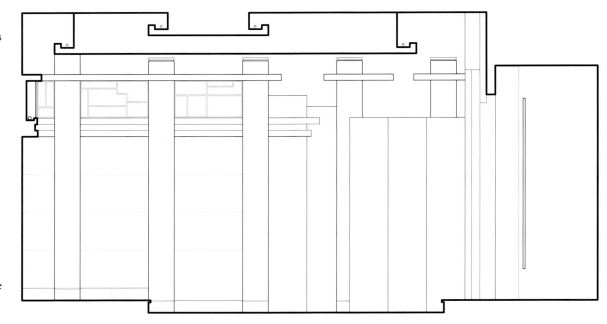

the hallway, the ceiling was lowered, and acoustical treatments and the equalization of a clever sound system helped achieve a more balanced sound in a very unbalanced space. Architectural elements such as the angled mahogany panels and multilevel ceiling soffit help to diffuse the sound as well. Audio harmony emerged from disharmony.

"This theater makes the experience equal to a state-of-the-art sound system," says DeGeorge. "And because it's surrounded by concrete, I can crank it and no sound [leaks] out."

DeGeorge likes contemporary movies and uses the theater several times a week. "It has a very warm feel. We can go in there with bathrobes and slippers. . . . We like big movies, and we recently bought the remastered version of *The Hustler*."

If ever there were a multilayered piece of filmmaking art, it would be *The Hustler*. Even on the screen here, what appears to be isn't quite. But that joy of discovery is felt before the curtains ever part. That's art.

The Mondrian-inspired lines in the mica light boxes
weave an orderly sort of asymmetry, as angled mahogany wall panels in the back of the room
help to balance the sound.

THE TUSCANY

ITALIAN COUNTRYSIDE
COMES TO THE GEORGIA COAST

One of the movie scenes Frank Argenbright likes to play for visitors to his home theater is from *Contact*, in which Jodie Foster ventures into alien territory. In an enthralling visual and audio sequence, she is hurtled through space and time, accelerating at warp speeds that bend the physics of light and sound.

It's a powerful scene, especially when viewed on a big screen and with big sound all around. The scene showcases the power of the Argenbrights' home theater and its prodigious audio and video systems, making you feel as if you're alongside Ms. Foster, anxiously embarking into the unknown.

Argenbright's visitors never have to enter a capsule to travel though space and time. By simply crossing the threshold to this home-entertainment space, they have journeyed to another place—and arrived in an old-world Tuscan village.

In the moment it takes to walk through the doors, the transport is complete. Step forward and a framework of rustic beams gives way to a twinkling star field and red-tile roofs, age-worn stone and mortar facades, peeling stucco that reveals stone and brickwork beneath, cypress trees and vines and even a working fountain. The space has that quaint patina of age, of a place that time has left behind.

This atmospheric auditorium
depicts an intimate Italian piazza, with even the proscenium
staged as a building.

Beyond the shuttered windows and through a stonework arch is a view of a hillside village imbued with a fiery sunset hue. It's that magic moment between day and night, the sky displaying its last warming rays amid remnant wisps of clouds, the stubborn spectrum of light casting the day, and indeed time, as if through a prism. Above, it fades to blue, then black, and a vast, endless star field of the sort you can view today only from those places untouched by progress. And it twinkles.

"I love the feeling of sitting out under the stars," says Argenbright. "It's a calming effect. It feels like you're in a park, with the windows of the buildings lit."

Distressed doors, rustic beams, peeling plaster, and a fountain (above) transport the owners to Tuscany. The doors on the left conceal the audio and video equipment.

The Tuscan decor matches the Mediterranean feel of the Argenbrights' coastal vacation home, from the cottages that greet visitors near the gate to the two-story wine tower down the hall to the room across from the home theater where they and their guests can enjoy a drink and get popcorn from an old-time popcorn machine.

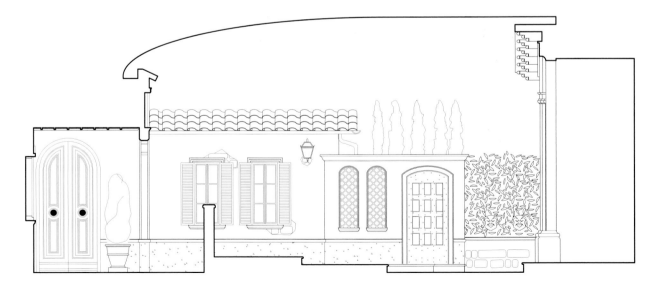

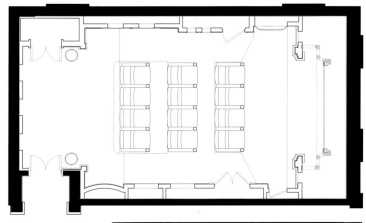

The inner workings are revealed, and a visible bank of theatrical lighting nods to the illusion that has been created.

Moreover, the theater's motif evokes places that are special to both Frank and Cathy Argenbright, though not necessarily for the times they have spent roaming the Tuscan countryside. Cathy went to high school in Atlanta, and her graduation ceremony was held in that city's old Fox Theater, an "atmospheric" theater famous for its Moorish facades and its twinkling star field with clouds that actually wisped across the sky. The Fox is something that Cathy holds dear, so when the Argenbrights decided to have a home theater, she wanted a similar feel with a twinkling night sky.

For Frank, the Tuscan theme recalls the time he spent in Florence studying art. The plazas, the streets, the timeless feel of a place so steeped in history and design echoes softly in the tones and textures of this theater. Long lit windows on one side evoke the city's understated architecture, while the leaded sidelights opposite hint at its medieval roots. A Palladian window above a set of wooden doors even casts a simple design with Florentine elegance.

The Argenbrights' guests are made to feel as if they have stepped into a true Tuscan piazza. Frank may offer up a movie scene or two, but he says the decor and feel of the space inspire many to suggest music instead.

Cathy savors *The Three Tenors*, appropriately framed in the stonework proscenium. And with its red-tile roof, the building makes it seem as if Pavarotti, Domingo, and Carreras are right there on stage, in an intimate Italian square.

Action movies make an impression on Frank, especially with a prodigious, top-of-the-line audiophile sound system consisting of powerful speakers concealed in the "stonework" and behind some of the windows to literally shake you in your seat. "There's no movie theater that I've been in that

These elegant doors are used to access speakers that fire through the windows

compares to it, other than an IMAX theater," says Frank. "When bullets ricochet, it feels like they're bouncing off the walls."

There is an element of Hollywood here. Those walls of supposed stone and brick and plaster were constructed at the studios of J. Frederick Construction in Connecticut, and assembled and displayed for the Argenbrights' review there before being disassembled and shipped south. To further the realistic sound of the theater, acoustic designer Steven Haas had to take into consideration all the materials in the facades when determining optimum speaker placement and the numerous acoustical treatments required for the sound system. A considerable amount of those treatments reside on the ceiling behind the curved fabric of the sky.

The effect of a vast night sky is enhanced by the 5,500 blinking fiber-optic lights that make it appear to twinkle. "It really does make you feel like you're outside," Frank says. "It's like Disney."

Unlike Disney, though, one backstage element is highly visible. On one building's roof, a profusion of

Faded brickwork and exposed beams provide a patina of time to our little village, a model of which is displayed in the theater as well.

stage lights illuminates the scene like a movie set. "It's a wink of an eye at the artificiality of the whole thing," says Theo Kalomirakis.

You see what you want to see in this theater—just as on the big screen, Jodie Foster's character completes her harrowing journey and sees all the wonderment of her wishes during her encounter with an alien world. Hers is a journey light-years into her soul. This one just takes you to Tuscany—and maybe, a bit beyond.

THE DIGITAL PALACE

THERE'S NO KEEPING UP WITH THE JONESES IN THIS THEATER

You could call Scott Jones a Renaissance man. His interests vary from astronomy to antiques to spending time with his kids. But a more accurate period description of him would be a turn-of-the-century man. Turn of the last century, that is. When Jones purchased and began renovating an English country house in Indiana, he made sure to preserve the details of its early 1900s look, from meticulously restoring the original woodwork to adding a great room of baronial splendor. Yet, all the while, he was making the old-world home a living laboratory of modern technology.

You see, in addition to living the life of an English country gentleman, Jones is a high-tech maven, a guru of modern technology who in the late 1980s developed the voice-mail system used by most telephone companies in the world. More recently, he built a home-entertainment electronics company called Escient Technologies.

Several years ago, Jones was in the middle of a major addition to his now 27,000-square-foot estate when Escient introduced its PowerPlay system, a 200-disc CD and DVD changer that allows you to play any disc at the touch of a button. And he decided that the best way to show off his company's new product would be to build a home theater.

Off a baronial great room
in this English country manor is an entry to different sort of
turn-of-the-century splendor.

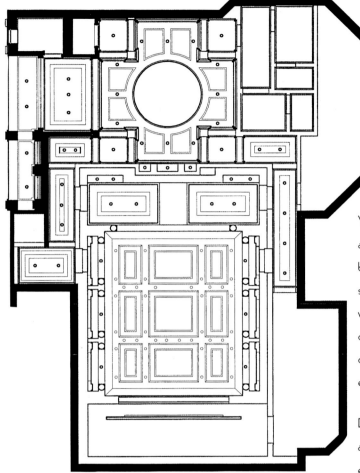

Of course, this was not to be any ordinary home theater. It was to be state-of-the-art, with all the latest and greatest technologies. And it had to match the turn-of-the-century look of his growing English country estate.

So upon entering the lobby to Jones's theater, you enter a near Victorian-style parlor of burgundy flowered wall panels and furnished with a rich rose sofa and a polished wooden bar. The only hints that this may be the lobby of a movie theater are the black-and-white framed photos of stars such as Greta Garbo and Fred Astaire. And the domed ceiling, which suggests something special is to come. "In the old days, the lobbies of theaters were designed to look like the living rooms and parlors of opulent homes, to give you that feeling of being in a very fine home," explains Theo Kalomirakis.

Doorways on either side of the bar lead to hallways and stairs, presenting an entrée to somewhere. Turn through the doors, and a different world exists. "Once you come down the stairs and into the theater, you are completely transported," Jones says.

Overlooking the theater from its balcony, one senses all the majesty of this home packaged in the most regal drama, as if you are ensconced in the box seat at a royal theatre. English-style chandeliers are framed by archways and columns, with silk brocade draped beyond. Corbel after corbel encircle the space, defining the formal structure. The coffered ceiling seemingly directs your attention to the large stage and towering curtains, the formality of the theater very nearly asking you to bow in deference. Something special is about to occur, indeed.

The lobby feels more like a Victorian parlor, the sofa and fabric walls combining with the stately lines and ceiling details to suggest something special to come.

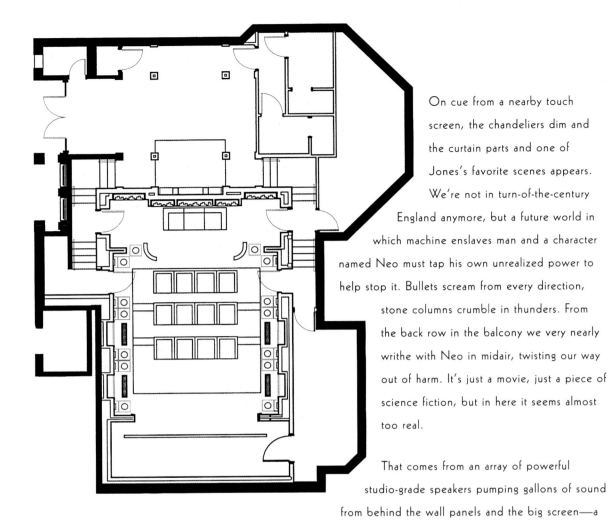

On cue from a nearby touch screen, the chandeliers dim and the curtain parts and one of Jones's favorite scenes appears. We're not in turn-of-the-century England anymore, but a future world in which machine enslaves man and a character named Neo must tap his own unrealized power to help stop it. Bullets scream from every direction, stone columns crumble in thunders. From the back row in the balcony we very nearly writhe with Neo in midair, twisting our way out of harm. It's just a movie, just a piece of science fiction, but in here it seems almost too real.

That comes from an array of powerful studio-grade speakers pumping gallons of sound from behind the wall panels and the big screen—a

The theater's design created the opportunity for multiple levels, including a balcony and entrance halls that descend several steps, prolonging the anticipation of entering a lavish auditorium.

sixteen-foot-wide screen that manages to display large-scale video in crisp filmlike images, thanks to a state-of-the-art device called an Interpolator—as well as an impressive list of amplifiers and control devices working behind the scenes, including those from Jones's former company.

The question is, is Jones a modern-day slave to technology, or has the master of this manor also mastered today's *Matrix* of man and machine?

For Jones, state-of-the-art technology makes all the difference. "The first time I saw *Moulin Rouge,* I saw it on a fifty- or sixty-inch TV, and I liked it," he says. "Then I saw it in this theater, and I saw so much

Entrance halls to the theater are accessed discreetly on either side of the bar and refreshment area.

more. I saw subtle glances on the dance floor and heard little phrases I didn't pick up on before. It has such an impact in this theater. You see and hear the movie exactly the way the director wanted it conveyed."

Jones's own production in building the theater was a model of efficiency, taking only a few months to complete the construction and installation of all the equipment. "We were far along in the house project and we had the foundation poured for the home theater, so we thought why not get it done for the product introduction," says Jones. "My father, who had been involved in building hospitals and other facilities, was the general contractor on the house, so we used some of the people he knew from building medical facilities, and with everyone else on the project, we got it done."

Through the first set of doors is a back-row balcony that has its own touch-screen controller (top center). The projector is housed in the enclosure above the balcony (left).

Jones decided to call his theater the Digital Palace, a play on words on the "electric palaces" that appeared in England after the turn of the twentieth century. The advent of films and their popularity in England inspired many to transform small shops into film houses, but the projectors were a fire hazard until a law mandated separate rooms to harness their power more safely. The age of England's opulent electric palaces, decorated to look like fine houses, was born.

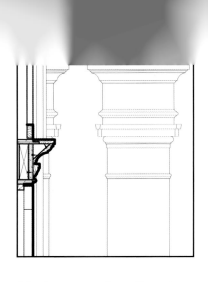

Nearly a century later, Scott Jones is harnessing, you could say harvesting, the power of technology in his own English manor home. He even films his children performing skits and plays on the theater stage, sending the video directly to his digital studio nearby. The video is later recorded to DVD and stored in an Escient PowerPlay DVD changer. Then he can call up any home movie by pressing a thumbnail photo of the scene on the theater's touch-screen controller.

With his 1900s home theater and mastery of this century's rapidly evolving technology, Scott Jones isn't just a man of the turn of the century. He's a man of two centuries.

The balcony provides a view fit for a king. The theater may look as if it's from another time, but it is endowed with cutting-edge audio and video systems.

SOUTH BEACH
ALL-STAR NIGHTS
IN SOUTH BEACH STYLE

Former baseball star Chili Davis owns the ultimate outdoor movie theater. On three sides are the famous buildings of Miami's South Beach, enclave of fast times, vibrant nights, and the architecture of a time that celebrated the flash and pizzazz of modern life.

Chili's theater isn't ringing with the din of South Beach's nightlife, however. It's peaceful and quiet. A sunset glow bathes the thirteen scale models of the Art Deco District's most legendary structures, as if they are somehow suspended in time.

There's the exuberant modernism of the Breakwater, the intricate cheerfulness of the Carlyle and the Hotel Collins Park, the soaring optimism of the Plymouth, the luscious curves of the Crescent, and the enduring styles of the Cameo, Shelborne, Delano, McAlpin, New Yorker, Ritz Plaza, Waldorf Towers, and Governor.

When Davis is sitting in one of the chairs, it's as if he is lying on that strip of perfect beach with the neon trim dancing on the horizon. And what a view it is, as the stars shine from the ceiling and he can call up several constellations of his choice. In a Capricorn mood? How about Scorpio or Cancer or the Big and Little Dippers?

*Miami monuments
such as the Breakwater and the Shelborne were lovingly re-created,
with a sunset glow painted behind.*

South Beach mainstays
the Carlyle, Ritz Plaza, and Collins Park give the owners the feeling
of sitting outside at night.

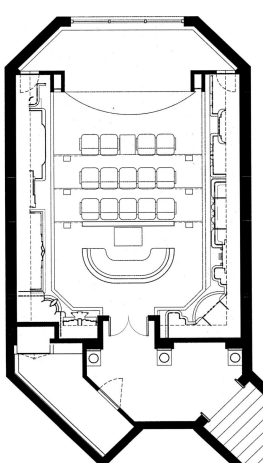

Lest we forget, there's a fair view toward the front of the theater when the movie images shine on the twelve-foot-wide screen. And when they don't, the retired slugger can gaze down upon another sun-drenched metropolis, the buildings of which resemble scale models next to his own.

In fact, you must turn your back on the theater to remember that you are not actually in Miami Beach, but on a desert hillside overlooking Phoenix, Arizona.

Chili Davis's South Beach wonderland was seven years in the making, a project that ebbed and flowed due to the demands of his baseball career and his own uncompromising sense of perfectionism. But it started with a simple thought. "I wanted to do a pretty grand theater," he recalls. "We were staying in New York and I was looking at the skyline, and I thought it would be great to do a theater with a skyline."

Manhattan's towering profile posed some problems, though. There was no way to capture the scale of those buildings in a one-story room. Davis also considered San Francisco, with a bridge located on either side of the sitting area. Then the breakthrough came when Theo Kalomirakis visited Miami Beach to help work on the restoration of a theater in the Art Deco District. "I was taken on a tour of the area, and I was bowled over by the colors and shapes and the style of architecture," Kalomirakis says. "I went back to Chili and told him that South

Beach would be better, because the scale is more intimate. Then we got every book available on the architecture in South Beach and studied them."

Once the buildings were selected, Kalomirakis's design team pored over the guidelines for each structure, studied the color schemes, even cut color samples from the actual buildings.

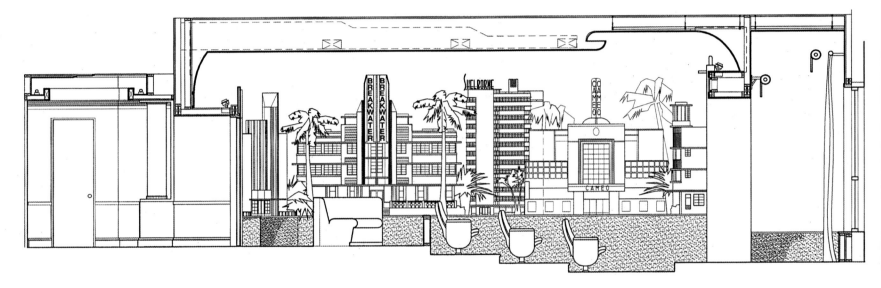

The material used to construct the buildings was computer-milled to cut the many windows. Once the buildings were constructed, the architectural details were added and the buildings painted to match those on South Beach.

Construction began on a new South Beach—this one in Connecticut, at the set design studios of J. Frederick Construction. Layouts of the buildings were computerized and the walls computer-milled to cut the many windows. The tiny mullions and sunshades and other Deco details were painstakingly applied. Finally, the buildings were shipped to Davis's home in Phoenix, reassembled, painted, and sometimes repainted as the real buildings in South Beach underwent their own renovations.

Much more than fine detail went into these buildings. In some cases, custom-made speakers reside behind the cloth windows to provide the room's powerful surround sound. In the rear, the Governor doubles as the theater's entry doors and houses a projector, which shines from one of the building's details.

For additional drama, precisely positioned theatrical lights highlight the buildings and enhance the soft glow of sunset painted on the walls

behind. The resulting look resembles the opening shot of the movie *The Birdcage*, as the camera glides over the water toward the pastel hue of Ocean Drive.

"The theater is my favorite part of the home," Davis says. "What I enjoy most about it is that it's a getaway." He likes to sequester himself there at times, lost to the outside world as he listens to some soft jazz and smokes a cigar—as if he were lounging under the stars of South Beach.

Later, the family can gather and entertain themselves with action movies or even performances on the intimate stage. Indeed, the joys of this theater are as diverse as the people of South Beach, each celebrating that place's unabashed joie de vivre. You'd never know they were separated by several decades and thousands of miles.

A projector shines from the Governor, which also doubles as the theater's doors. Custom-made speakers are concealed within several of the buildings.

THE LUNADA SUNSET

TRADITIONAL FRENCH AND
THE SOFT GLOW OF L.A.

Sometimes Jeanie Blum sits on a cliff near her home in Southern California and savors the soft hues ending a Lunada Bay day. She doesn't have the opportunity to do this often, as her business creating Hawaiian escapes for others occupies much of her life.

Blum loves doing for others. And so her very successful business keeps her busy satisfying the travel needs of her clients. Yet when she's sitting on that cliff, "I actually forget about everything," she says. "When the sun goes down and I see all those beautiful colors, it gives me the most peaceful feeling."

It's the same feeling, she recalls, of being a schoolgirl and venturing to the Uptown or Chicago Theater in her hometown of the same name, and gazing in wonderment at the ornate details and lavish decor. "I used to look at everything around me in the theater. With all the gold and the burgundy, you felt like you were in Vienna. Now you don't have that when you go to a theater."

So when Blum decided to build a Mediterranean-style villa near Lunada Bay and saw a magazine article about a Theo Kalomirakis—designed home theater named the Uptown, those memories rushed back and she embraced them. "I wanted something to fit with the Mediterranean feel of the home, and I wanted a classic and traditional look like the old Uptown in Chicago," she says. "I like the vintage type of theaters that are very classical and romantic."

The lobby radiates a warm, classic touch with its gold dome, gold-leaf console, and fabric wall panels.

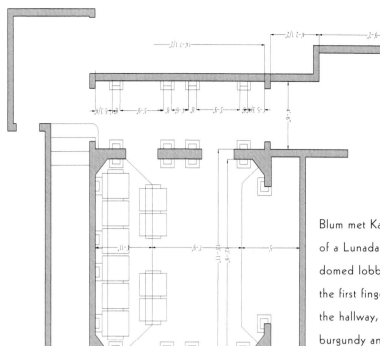

Blum met Kalomirakis by the Pacific, and the idea of incorporating the feel of a Lunada sunset struck. Visitors can sense it in the golden glow of the domed lobby, and in the soft pink tone of the fabric floral wall panel, as if the first fingers of dusk have begun exploring the sky. Through the doors to the hallway, the glow intensifies with a rich golden light and touches of burgundy and rose. The formal columns and their Ionic capitals and archways are even trimmed in a golden hue.

Through the archways is the sunburst of the theater, its deep tones of burgundy and gold in the curtain, the seats, the wall panels, the violet coffered ceiling—as if it is that magic moment when sun meets horizon and paints the sky. It's that moment we want to grasp and preserve, but are fortunate if it merely lingers before dissipating into dark.

For Jeanie Blum, this theater has managed to grasp something from her past that she had thought was gone. "It's the same feeling as sitting on the cliff and watching the sunset," she says. "Sitting in this theater, I go back as a child and remember the good times. Building a business on my own, I forgot to enjoy my life, but this theater brought back that sense of excitement."

Blum admits to being a hopeless romantic, some of her favorite films being *Gone With the Wind, Doctor Zhivago,* and *Casablanca,* which she can enjoy now in the traditional decor reminiscent of the Chicago movie palaces from her youth.

The side hall offers an arched glimpse into the French traditional-style theater. The equipment rack, however, remains deftly concealed.

Don't think that Blum just sits in her theater misty-eyed at thought of romantic could-have-beens. The theater also enables her to entertain her

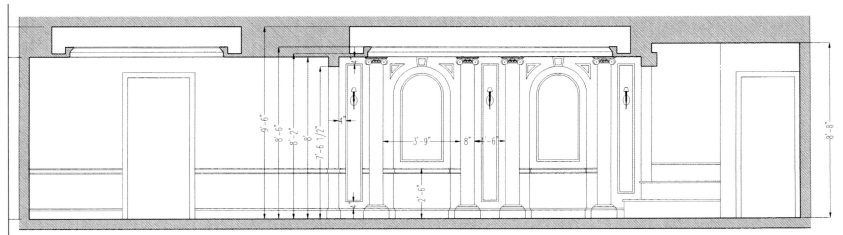

Architectural details and decor sing of the classical. Even the contemporary pleasure of a snack bar features espresso elegance of old.

frequent guests in style. "When I entertain, everyone usually ends up in the theater," she says. "It's such a great place, you forget you're in a house and think you're in a real, old-fashioned movie theater.

"And my family and friends love to eat, so we have a concession stand in the back with popcorn and hot dogs, because in Chicago we love to eat good hot dogs." There's also an espresso machine to satisfy her more contemporary craving for caffeine. Even that casts a golden hue.

For Jeanie Blum, this sunset doesn't mark the lingering end of a day. For her, this Lunada Sunset is a brilliant and beautiful beginning.

THE TOLEDO

CLASSIC MOORISH STYLE SET IN NORTHERN CALIFORNIA

The high-tech entrepreneur who owns this home lives in a global village. Seven different languages can be spoken in his household. So when he and his family relocated to Northern California, he wanted a house reflecting the area's Spanish heritage. The owner's ancestors had lived in Spain during the Middle Ages, near the then-innovative capital of Toledo, so he was interested in Spanish Colonial architecture that had some Moorish influence.

There weren't many true Spanish Colonial homes in the areas where he was looking, but he found one that had been constructed in the 1920s in the Spanish Revival style of the 1700s. The house had been built by a pair of innovative thinkers of their day, the husband an author of novels concerning social issues and the wife a feminist and well-known writer. The wife was one of the highest-paid women of her time, and the couple used their Spanish-style casa to entertain celebrities from New York and Hollywood.

"One room was a billiards room that the husband had built against the wishes of his wife," the current owner says. "And I thought it would be a fantastic room for a theater."

Descend the steps through the tunnel to the theater, and you sense both the Spanish Colonial heritage and something about the present owners. It's as if you're in the cooling confines of a hacienda en route to a dug-out hideaway—a wine cellar, perhaps—but on the cavern ceiling are highlighted constellations of Leo and Libra, the Zodiac signs of the owner's two sons. Enter the stone archway and you are in a Moorish palace, lush with rich colors and textures and many more geometric designs in the ceilings, the walls, and a proscenium recalling intricate Moorish tile work. "There is geometry within the geometry," the owner says. "There are layers of geometry in the theater."

Hexagons and squares adorn the ceiling, stars and swirls blend to form diamonds and squares and triangles in the mesmerizing grating along the side walls, and all the patterns seemingly combine in the colorful proscenium. The overall effect creates a feeling that there is more here than meets the eye—that if you take the effort to look hard, you will be deeply rewarded. "In Moorish design, the geometric patterns can be perceived in a number of different ways," says the owner.

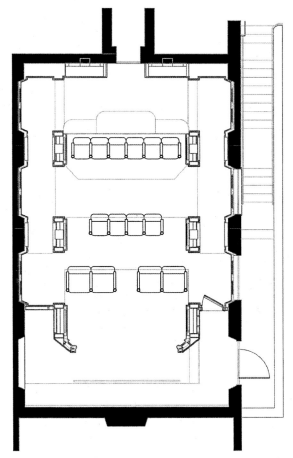

Like intricate Moorish tile work, patterns within patterns—such as these on the chandeliers and ceiling—excite the eye.

The existing room was even dug down to accommodate cinema-style seating for twenty-one, with an entire wall removed to make room for the heavy equipment. That was no easy task, considering that the home is on the National Register of Historic Places and doing virtually anything to the exterior requires approvals.

The ceiling vaults and wall grating provide a plush and palatial texture.

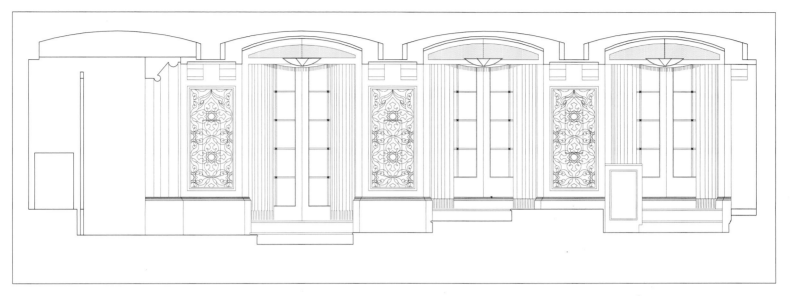

Guests enter through a tunnel and stone archway, which reveal little of the treasure that lies beyond.

That was just the beginning of the challenges in building a theater room in this historic home. "There were a lot of challenges in the geometry of the room," the owner recalls. Theo Kalomirakis designed the theater to fit the existing space, which featured multiple vaults in the ceiling, for one thing. Other parts of the ceiling were trimmed with dark wood beams to match the exposed beams in the rest of the house and create a seamless look.

Grilles designed for the side of the theater conceal loudspeakers, and the many theater elements are positioned to the inch to achieve the right balance of look and performance. "The room is very harmonious with the rest of the house," says the owner, "but once you go through that tunnel, you are transported."

The owner and his family entertain frequently in the theater and watch everything from cartoons to action

movies to classics. But the most memorable moment, he says, was the day they turned it on. Even this technology innovator was impressed. "I was stunned by how vivid the images were. It really does suspend your disbelief," he says.

One can go virtually anywhere in the world in this theater. It's equipped to play video formats from Europe and elsewhere, so in the tradition of his ancestors and his house, he and his family can continue life in a global village—with some technology and geometry and intellectual heritage mixed in.

The French doors lead to a courtyard, and the assortment

of design elements conspire to form one pleasing and exotic whole.

THE RITZ
A SHOWCASE FOR ART AND DECO
SOPHISTICATION

There is something about the Hollywood of yesteryear that makes us want to grasp and preserve it, as if doing so will return it to us. Certainly it was a simpler and more innocent time. Filmmakers enjoyed more latitude in their storytelling, their celluloid creations seeming to shine that much brighter in black and white. Famous actors and actresses weren't just revered as white-hot stars and cultural icons, but held up as shining examples of how we should live and *act* in our own lives.

But there is a much deeper yearning in our appeal for the Hollywood of the past. Many of us today feel an unabated nostalgia for the class and sophistication of that time, which has all but disappeared amid today's media frenzy.

The spotlights of yesteryear certainly shone brightly on its most successful stars. They wore glamorous fashions, they enjoyed the best that life had to offer, but there was something refined about it, something evident in both the films and their lifestyles that didn't reveal all in the spirit of the current day's glam parade. Something was left for the imagination, whether it was a bedroom door closing in front of lovers or the media's comportment to leave the private lives of the prominenti politely behind their own doors.

The entrance blares of Deco, but what lies beyond relives the refined style and elegance of a time past.

In this case, you could call Martin and Janet Smith throwbacks to that time. They're not Hollywood stars. They don't even live near Hollywood, but in the suburbs of Dallas. They're not famous; they eschew the spotlight. And although they love the finer things in life and possess a true passion for having the best, they don't flaunt it. The thing they treasure the most is their privacy.

So as you pass by the limestone facade and beneath the marquee of the Ritz, you are entering a special, very private space. And, as the flares of the cast-bronze Art Deco doors strongly suggest, a space appointed with tender care to evoke the glamour and refinement of another time.

Through the exquisite doors is a gallery of Hollywood gods from Judy Garland to Johnny Weissmuller, all life-size and lifelike.

"The whole reason we did the cinema was for privacy, so we don't have to go out for entertainment," Martin says. As the Smiths' trusted interior designer, Hershel Cannon, explains, "Martin sees this house as a respite. It's a place he doesn't have to leave if he doesn't want to."

One enters this special place via a long hall, its shining terrazzo floor stretching through sections delineated by limestone columns with bronze claddings, each segment adorned by life-size posters of stars from cinema past. They seem almost larger than life, up there on the walls, but in truth they aren't. They very nearly seem to come back to life.

Before venturing farther into this space, it should be noted here that this entire house is not as it seems from the outside. That is because everything in it, though done in the Smiths' spirit of having and being the best, is entirely without ostentation. From the street, this is another nice house in a nice suburb. But step inside, and it becomes so much more. It exudes the

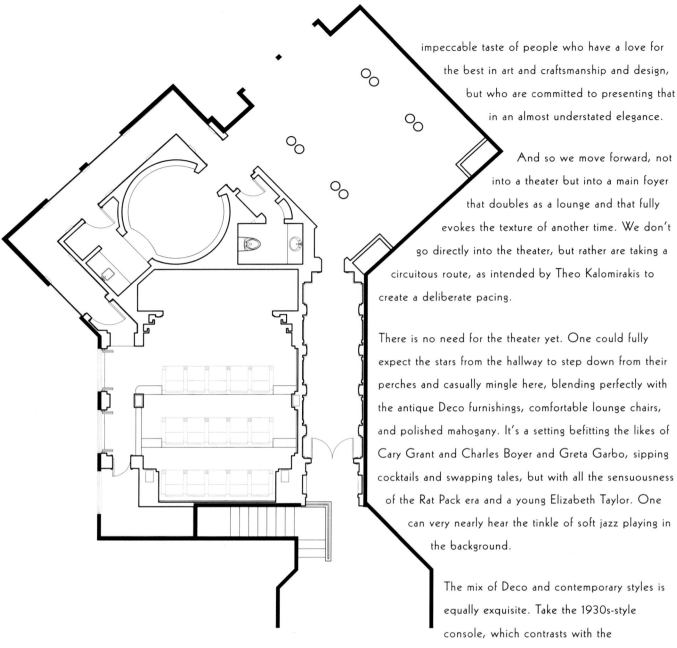

impeccable taste of people who have a love for the best in art and craftsmanship and design, but who are committed to presenting that in an almost understated elegance.

And so we move forward, not into a theater but into a main foyer that doubles as a lounge and that fully evokes the texture of another time. We don't go directly into the theater, but rather are taking a circuitous route, as intended by Theo Kalomirakis to create a deliberate pacing.

There is no need for the theater yet. One could fully expect the stars from the hallway to step down from their perches and casually mingle here, blending perfectly with the antique Deco furnishings, comfortable lounge chairs, and polished mahogany. It's a setting befitting the likes of Cary Grant and Charles Boyer and Greta Garbo, sipping cocktails and swapping tales, but with all the sensuousness of the Rat Pack era and a young Elizabeth Taylor. One can very nearly hear the tinkle of soft jazz playing in the background.

The mix of Deco and contemporary styles is equally exquisite. Take the 1930s-style console, which contrasts with the contemporary custom-made lounge chairs in color alone. Kalomirakis found the console, its clean lines and form setting the tone for the room. The lounge chairs, says interior designer Cannon, were made from fiddleback pommele that was cut on the diagonal and upholstered in chocolate mohair with a silver thread to add the subtlest glitz. The mirrored table was custom-made, based on another that Cannon and Smith had seen and liked.

Guests are led on a circuitous route to the theater, first encountering the long gallery, the lounge, and the monkey bar.

A René Lalique sconce dating from the late 1920s greets guests to the retro lounge and main foyer.

The lounge exudes comfort, class, and sophistication
in the spirit of Hollywood glamour of the past. You can almost hear ice tinkling in the glass
and jazz tickling your ear.

Mahogany columns frame a mix of antique Art Deco and contemporary furnishings, including an Osvaldo Borsani console from the early 1930s, Nancy Corzine armless chairs, and custom-crafted contemporary lounge chairs.

The silver thread in the mohair, the mirrored table, the window sheers that cast a Hollywood blue into the room—all add just the right light and touch to this elegantly glamorous space. Add the Nancy Corzine bench and armless chairs, and the gap between Deco and contemporary is bridged as if this era of Hollywood never left us.

"Martin is the kind of guy who wants the best," says Cannon. "And he wants it to exude sheer class and sophistication." Smith brings that passion to his various

The "monkey bar" mural by Artgroove provides some color, whimsy, and a sense of pure innocence and fun, while the terrazzo floor retains Deco styling.

collections, be it that of his prized Ferraris, which some of his neighbors may not know he even has, his wines, or his works of art.

The Smiths' house is a mix of great art, deftly showcasing works from the sixteenth century to original early Picasso drawings to a twenty-two-piece set of pre-Columbian jade displayed in the nearby powder room. No space escapes an artistic touch here. On the antique Deco console is a set of four bronzes, providing yet another eclectic touch.

On a more whimsical note is the mural in what is called the monkey bar, a circular room with a Deco-starred floor and a sweeping impression of a jungle scene. Monkeys swing from vines and trees in this colorful acrylic-on-canvas that was inspired by a circular mural

done by Pierre Bourdelle in 1933. Bourdelle's mural depicts animals in carved and lacquered linoleum panels and still exists outside the women's lounge of Cincinnati's very Art Deco Union Terminal railroad station.

The flora and fauna of the jungle motif cast the bar room in a playful light, setting it somewhat apart from the more sophisticated look of the lounge, while grounding all presumed taste and style in a natural, vibrant, even somewhat primal scene. This is where the Rat Pack might gather for drinks and jokes and impromptu dulcet tones.

At the proper pace, we come, at last, to the home theater, where if the Smiths still want contemporary entertainment, they can enjoy it in the grand style of the Art Deco and Hollywood past. All the cool sophistication, Deco stylings, and whimsical yet grounded artwork continue in this space. In fact, many of the elements from the hall, lounge, and bar areas come together in the theater in a crescendo of high style, with an added flair for the filmlike fantastic.

The owners' passion for art is also showcased in

a collection of valuable pieces displayed in the powder room (left).

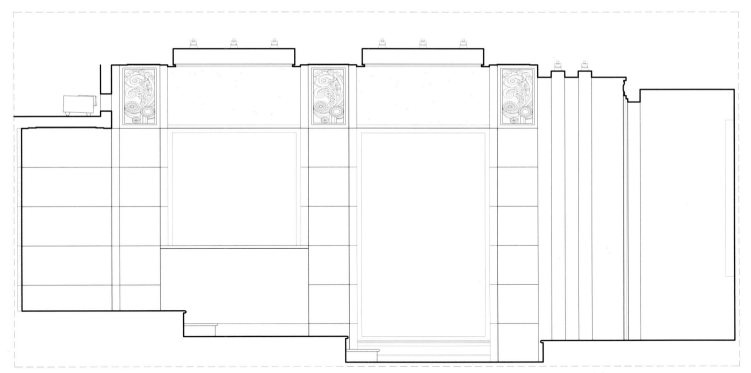

The theater shows more of a flair for the dramatic, with its intricate backlit ceiling and column grilles. The murals are outlined with gold to appear when the lights go down.

The cast-bronze and backlit ceiling panels provide the most elaborate touch. The feeling is repeated in the backlit floral wall panels. They top the more contemporary-looking mahogany columns and provide a transition to the frieze of artwork done in the same whimsical style and colors of the monkey bar.

This art, however, is different, the side panels reinterpreting Paul Manship's bronze sculptures of man and woman among *The Four Elements*: earth, wind, water, and fire. The Smiths, it seems, remain grounded in nature even in this more elaborate space. Yet the proscenium at the front of the room is lit in the same Hollywood hue as the lounge windows, and framed with claddings of a smaller version to those found in the hallway.

Care was taken with the highest-quality audio and video equipment as well. For example, custom-made speakers were located and fitted by systems installer HomeTronics to a tiny degree of tolerance, allowing virtually no margin for error.

The theater brings this glamour and refinement and passion for quality together in an elegant and lively space, also conveying in its more flamboyant touches the fantasy world of watching great films, past or

Surround speakers in the rear corners
are concealed with cloth grilles; they had to be positioned exactly so they wouldn't
interfere with the theater's designs.

present. All this comes, of course, with a feel of entrée into a world like that of Hollywood past.

Artgroove murals in the theater reinterpret Paul Manship's Four Elements in a style and coloring similar to those of the monkey bar. These show fire and water.

"The Smiths' home is a very private thing," explains Cannon, "though the cinema is not just there for their entertainment, but for them to invite other people into the home for a completely unique experience."

Throughout the home, all the artwork is highlighted, and at night it creates a mystical environment. But it is what it is, and there is no element of illusion. "If you're fortunate enough to be one of the invited few, you come away with an appreciation of what was done in this home," says Cannon. "So few people can go into a private residence and have the pleasure of seeing the real thing."

Isn't that, after all, what tickles our nostalgia for eras past? We gaze back to a time when we could be the very best and enjoy the very best and yet maintain our privacy while doing all that. We yearn for the time when being glamorous meant possessing something more in human substance and something less in sound bites and popularity ratings. That is the very private glamour and soaring dignity of this sophisticated space.

THE SIFNOS

CRUISING THE GREEK ISLES IN CONTEMPORARY STYLE

You could call Nicolas A. Vernicos a learned family man. His family and friends have endowed him with the knowledge to operate a large business, enjoy the power of entertainment, and love art. Vernicos represents the fourth generation of a long-standing maritime enterprise, the Vernicos Shipping Group, which provides vessels for yachting, oceangoing shipping—the works. So when it was time to construct a home theater in his family's seaside home near Athens, it was only natural that the theme would be nautical, though with a contemporary twist.

Vernicos learned some valuable lessons from a home theater that he and his wife, Barbara, had in the living room of their previous home. Barbara wanted to conceal the screen in the room, so the couple commissioned a contemporary artist to produce sliding fiberglass panels that open to reveal the screen. "That is when I became a contemporary art collector," says Vernicos.

A high-tech nautical theme was interpreted

in light boxes that recall portholes, and a stainless-steel pilaster contains

a speaker and lighting controls.

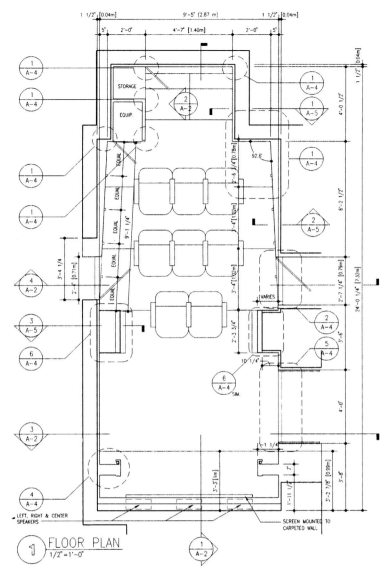

FLOOR PLAN
1/2" = 1'-0"

Perforated waves of stainless steel lap at the ceiling in this cozy family space, itself a piece of contemporary art.

He and Barbara learned that a home theater should be in a dedicated space, so that those who want to watch a movie after dinner can do so and those who don't can do other things. "I also realized that home entertainment is the best tool to keep the family together," Vernicos says. He and Barbara have three children, now ages sixteen to twenty-four.

Vernicos first learned the power of entertainment from a schoolmate whose father was Spyros Skouras, then president at 20th Century-Fox. "I would often be invited to their home on the weekend to see a film that wasn't being released until Monday," he recalls. "This really instilled in me a big interest in movies."

The dedicated theater room in the new Vernicos home reflects a nautical theme in a dramatic, contemporary style. It's not a large space, but it exudes the intimate feel of a yacht cabin and of time shared with family and friends. The polished-wood panels are interspersed with numerous lights that recall portholes, as waves of perforated stainless steel lap at the ceiling. Even the name of the theater reflects the nautical heritage of the family, which hails from the seafaring island of Sifnos, one of the Cyclades group in the Aegean Sea.

The family provides guests with a special feeling of their own. At the entrance is a work of contemporary art in the form of a scrolling electronic marquee, which is used to welcome people to the home and display the title of the movie that's playing.

Best of all, says Vernicos, on weekend and holidays the children can bring their friends here and enjoy a good time without going out. Happy sailing.

EXPANDING
HORIZONS

EXPANDING HORIZONS
THEMATIC ARCHITECTURE DESIGNS
FOR THE HOME

A home theater may provide a lavish escape, but it remains just one part of our total entertainment, one slice of the way we can use our homes to nourish our senses and revitalize our souls. And so some of Theo Kalomirakis's clientele have asked him to design other parts of their homes, from cafés to wine cellars to bowling alleys.

Kalomirakis has responded by extending his thematic designs beyond the home theater, beyond the lobby and box office and marquee—to produce thematic entertainment spaces that reflect much more of his clients' lives. After all, when creating a personal fantasy, why stop at the theater doors?

These entertainment complexes feature entire streetscapes with storefronts that display the owners' most cherished collections but more importantly, showcase the ways in which they choose to enrich their lives.

One owner strolls down memory lane in a Main Street from the town of his youth, complete with his collection of classic automobiles from that era, a dairy-bar café, a jewelry store—and yes, a theater. Another savors the rich tastes of a French country village, lined with cobblestones and featuring a wine shop, a pen store, a toy store with a working toy train, and much more; the village contains an elaborate theater as well.

These themed entertainment spaces don't only tickle the imaginations of their owners and their guests. They don't only rejuvenate and refresh. The total transport they provide to other times and places makes their owners' great escapes complete.

THE RIALTO

Frank Wilson is a tinkerer and a builder. He engrosses himself in projects, sometimes for days, sometimes for years. Whether he's fixing and restoring his collection of classic automobiles, learning how to use new tools in his custom woodshop, building a successful networking software company, or creating a trip down memory lane, his projects have provided some interesting twists and turns in his life.

Wilson wasn't satisfied with having just a home theater in this contemporary home made up entirely of curves, and so the 2,500-square-foot entertainment space features a café and dairy bar, a jewelry store, an automobile showroom, a wine cellar, and even a bowling alley—much of it recalling his hometown of Charleston, West Virginia.

Stroll down this lane, and you encounter the Rialto theater that used to be on Charleston's Quarrier Street, the Blossom Dairy that is still there today, and the Kay's Jewelers storefront. Add an automobile showroom and a bowling alley, and you can do the Charleston right there—in coastal California, that is.

"I've always been a project guy. This was my project, and I finished the project, and it came out just as I envisioned it," Wilson says. Working with Theo Kalomirakis helped Wilson realize the streetscape design, and along the way Kalomirakis created his first thematic home-entertainment complex, expanding far beyond the scope of home theaters, even the ones with lavish lobbies and ticket counters and elaborate marquees.

The inspiration for the theater
comes from a hometown memory, the starred terrazzo floor from Hollywood, and the vitrolite walls
from coloring the glass from the rear.

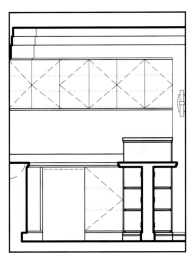

The vision behind the complex didn't develop right away, though. Wilson took years to oversee the building of his striking 30,000-square-foot contemporary California home, built entirely of supple curves and appropriately called *Portabello*. And the project had some twists and turns of its own.

The size of the home was partly intended to house Wilson's collection of twenty classic cars that he likes to drive. But this personal project within a project arose when he and his wife decided to include a home theater. The couple have two teenage daughters, so they also wanted to include a recreation space for the girls to entertain friends and grab something to eat without having to go upstairs.

"That blossomed into having a café for the kids downstairs and a soda fountain, but we didn't want a fifties style to it. We wanted something more flowing than cute, so we started looking at theaters with cafés nearby that we could go into after watching a movie," Wilson recalls.

"Then I started thinking of my hometown of Charleston, and how we used to go to the Blossom Dairy café after school, and how the Rialto Theater was right down the street," he says. "When you get to be my age, you start looking back at the era when you were young and feel the nostalgia of it all." In fact, this year Wilson revisited Charleston to reminisce with his schoolmates at their forty-fifth high-school class reunion.

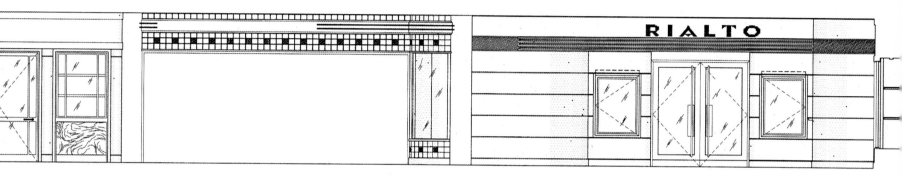

The jewelry store showcases pieces from the owner's family and features a vault door purchased from a local bank.

He doesn't have to travel far to recall his younger days, though. Stroll down this home's memory lane, and you'll be transported to the place of Wilson's youth, with some modern-day touches, of course. And along the way, you'll be entertained and surprised, and you'll experience some of the arc of a person's life.

At one end of the lane, you'll likely encounter one or two of the cars from Wilson's youth displayed in Frank's Motor Works. It could be his 1957 fuel-injection Corvette, it could be one of only 550 1953 Cadillac Eldorados that were made, or it could be a 1957 BMW 507 roadster paired with the new Z8 roadster, a combination Wilson put together because both were featured in recent television commercials. It could even be one of the few famous Tuckers in existence.

If you're really lucky, you may glimpse the prize of Wilson's collection: a pair of silver 1957 Mercedes-Benz 300SLs: the famous Gullwing version, with the doors that open vertically, and the roadster, which was

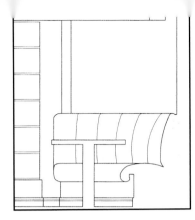

available in silver only as a special order. Both also have knock-off fifth wheels, making them an exceptionally rare combination. A famous collector gave Wilson the idea to collect the two cars. "He had a pair, though he painted his roadster silver," Wilson says. "So I sought out the pair." It was another project of sorts for Wilson, so he found a special-order silver roadster and had it restored.

Wilson is passionate about his automobiles, though he has slowed down. He used to race vintage cars on tracks such as Sears Point and Laguna Seca in California. "I raced until I was sixty, until I decided I would either kill myself or kill someone else," he says. So now he concentrates on building and enjoying his collection of classic cars.

Behind the showroom is the garage, which can house fifteen cars, and he has a car elevator so cars can be brought in and out.

Next to the Motor Works, Wilson displays some other jewels in Kay's Jewelers, the store's marquee appearing just as it did years ago in Charleston. The idea behind this storefront isn't to sell jewelry, however. "The

The café brings a fifties-style soda fountain into the cappuccino-bar age with rich, cherry tones. There's also a nod to deli-style celebrity walls.

The mural above the banquette recalls the owner's upbringing in Charleston, West Virginia.

whole idea of the place is to store your mother's or grandmother's jewelry and keep it in a nice place instead of packing it up in a box," says Wilson. "And lucky for me, my wife's middle name is Kay."

In the store, handsome cherry and glass cases display jewelry and objets d'art, inviting visitors to browse leisurely. One almost expects a well-dressed clerk to appear behind the counter and offer assistance. Perhaps the biggest sparkle in this giant trinket box comes from the large vault door, complete with massive hinges and metal latches signifying that something special lies beyond.

Next door is the Blossom Dairy café, with a sign that Wilson says is a replica of the one from the Charleston shop, now called the Blossom Deli. The sign's Broadway-style lettering and backdrop of glass blocks hint at something fun and whimsical. Inside you won't find the fifties-style chrome and colors of Charleston's legendary eatery and soda fountain, but a more modern, luxurious take on the café experience, with polished cherry

Dessert, anyone? The owners' daughters use the café to mix and sip milk shakes— just like the good old days.

woods in the chairs and stools as well as subdued lighting more closely resembling that of a cappuccino bar.

There are hints of those wholesome dairy-time days. Peer into the display case, and samples of milk shakes and desserts exude all the innocence of an old-time dairy bar. The diner-like tables are even trimmed in chrome.

Touches of Charleston and the Mountain State are present as well, in the deep blue upholstery and floors that Wilson insisted on because the West Virginia state colors are blue and gold. There's even a blue-seated booth like the ones in today's Blossom Dairy, only this is a fabric-backed banquette in an alcove with

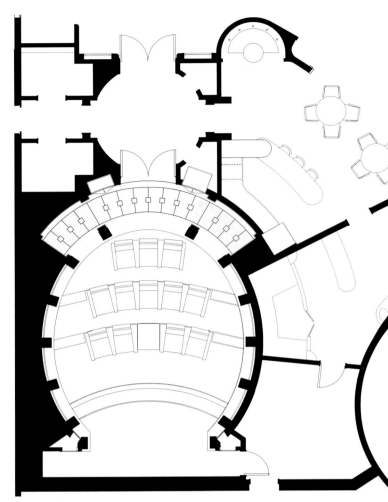

Deco-style curves in the frieze above and a magazine rack within reach. The entire effect manages at once to cross several decades of generations and styles.

The biggest hint of West Virginia is in the mural above the banquette, depicting scenes from Wilson's youth in Charleston, including portraits of the statehouse; Wilson's Stonewall Jackson High School, with an inset of Jackson above; the city's Rock Lake Pool, which was once a quarry and has been replicated outside this modern home; and even the house where Wilson grew up.

The café may not look exactly like the Blossom Deli of today or even yesteryear, but it's hard for Wilson not to feel as if he's reliving his youth. "It's always nice to look at that mural and remember all the good times, even the not-so-good times," he says.

The café isn't just a showpiece. It's also functional, with working appliances and refrigerator and a sink. "The kids love it," says Melanie Wilson. "They use it to make milk shakes." It seems that the good old days may not be so far away after all.

The theater slowly reveals itself like a Fabergé egg. Note the locations of the jewelry store and café (top right).

Outside and across the blue-skied hallway is a glass-walled view of the grotto, which recalls Charleston's Rock Lake Pool, and the entrance to the two-alley Beach Bowling Lanes. There wasn't a Beach Bowling Lanes in Charleston, but this pays tribute to the family's love of the beach. The signage glows Deco, and next to it is an advertisement for five-cent Coca-Colas— remember those?—which gives way to the ticket booth and the Deco brilliance of Charleston's Rialto theater.

The Rialto in the West Virginia capital is no longer standing, but here it is brought back to life with a

The theater follows the house rules for curves. Even the door handles are pleasingly bowed.

The small lobby of the theater is unadorned, yet it casts an almost futuristic feel of being transported elsewhere.

blaring neon marquee, the brilliant canopy of
incandescent lights used at the time, and, like any
institution reincarnated in Southern California, a little
touch of Tinsel Town. On the terrazzo floor are

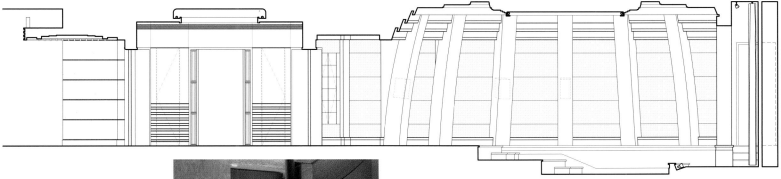

Hollywood stars forming a mini-Walk of Fame. They're
aligned, of course, with abstracted bands of spotlights
emanating from the entrance doors.

Once inside, memories of Charleston and the fifties are
all but left behind. The lobby is a perfect circle,
unadorned with furnishings but beholding the sandy hue
of a wavy burled maple-wood grain that gives one the
feeling of floating within the space. Above is a brilliant
white dome, and at your feet a blue-and-gold carpet
with the Rialto's "R" at the center of a spiraled sunburst.
It feels almost as if you're inside some science-fiction
transporter, as if the room is about to spin you into a
different dimension.

It's only a prelude of what's to come. In fact, this
entire entertainment complex has been but an introduction to what is to come. Visitors can exit a side
door back into the café, but you feel compelled to
venture deeper through the double doors—to see what
new world awaits.

This theater is all about drama. It is a womb of a room, egg-shaped with a true arch of a proscenium and lined with massive ribs of columns supporting a stepped circular frieze, the columns and frieze all made of Japanese ash, a wondrous wood with a large, free-flowing, amoeba-like grain, the type of which was only hinted at in the circular lobby. The wood encircles the ceiling and a circular light structure with spotlights against blue and gold. The deep blue seats and curtain add to the sensation of a floating calm.

"There's not a straight line or wall in the whole house, so we were looking for more of an oval-shaped theater," says Wilson. "We were looking at theaters from the 1930s and 1940s. We probably looked at about ten theaters or so, and Theo found one that had a similar look to this one."

What Kalomirakis found was the circular theater that Joseph Urban designed for the New School in New York in 1935, with a dramatic arched proscenium and stepped-dome ceiling. Urban was an architect and set

designer also known for designing the dramatic and oval Ziegfeld Theater in New York.

Wilson says the teenagers use the theater frequently for viewing movies and playing video games on the big screen, and the couple sees a few movies there each month as well. Wilson also likes it to watch sports, specifically Pac-10 college teams during the "March Madness" of the annual NCAA men's basketball tournament. But the Wilsons intend the theater to be used for a lot more.

The men's and ladies' rooms feature elegant, Deco-style sconces, mirrors, and fixtures. The attention to detail shows in the signage, the objets d'art, and the color schemes.

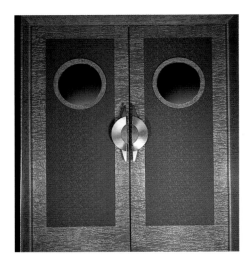

Wilson says he had footlights installed in front of the large, curved stage so his grandchildren someday could use it to perform, or to enjoy the performances of others. There's even a backstage entrance through a wine cellar, which is the secret room behind the vault door in Kay's Jewelers.

Off the circular lobby of the Rialto are his-and-her washrooms, decorated in the rich Art Deco style and beautifully adorned with Deco-style sconces and mirrors and other luxurious period accoutrements. Virtually no detail went unnoticed.

Although he considers himself more of a big-picture rather than detailed guy, Wilson took a keen interest in many of the details in this entertainment complex. "I am detailed when it comes to things in my home, such as what color carpet you're going to put down and what fixtures you're going to put in the bathrooms," he says.

This project of Wilson's may be complete, but it has spawned another that he's tinkering with in his woodshop. "This entire house was designed on

The oval theater is based on Joseph Urban's design
for the New School auditorium in New York, which was built in the 1930s.

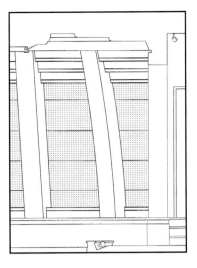

computer, and I have two CAD-CAM (computer-aided design, computer-aided manufacturing) computer stations in my woodshop. I'm taking up CAD-CAM as a hobby and using it to design three-dimensional art objects made out of wood. I'm taking lessons in CAD-CAM, and I'm going to figure out how to computerize the milling of the wood for those objects," Wilson says. "I like using new technologies with traditional materials, and I want to use this more as an art form, especially when I retire."

That is, if he can leave his ongoing software-company project alone. The computerized woodworking will be the latest in a series of happy turns in his life. This memorable place echoes just a few of them.

*The blue chairs, curves, and free-flowing grain
of Japanese ash create a relaxing sensation in a dramatic space.*

THE PARAMOUNT

PROVENCE IN PEBBLE BEACH

Would you like a taste of rural France? This homeowner did, though he didn't limit his appetite to a French-style theater. His intent was to re-create an entire village from Provence, where the tastes of everything seem just a little richer. The wine sips as if it flows directly from vine to bottle to glass, the cheese has a sharpness and almost fluid texture, even the air is laced with an earthy flavor that doesn't connote the rustic as much as the luxury of the way things should really taste and feel. Breathe deep and savor it.

Provence is a connoisseur's delight, and so is this themed wing of a rural French village, replicated in its cobblestone paths and stone walls and wooden doors, and infused with the interests and collections of the homeowner. This new-old version of rural France in coastal California contains a cigar shop, a wine shop, a toy store, a stationery shop for a pen collection, even a grocery and public rest rooms—not to mention an elaborate, elegant theater.

The theater shines brightly, but this entertaining space also features a wine shop and several other attractions.

Venture down the cobblestone ways and you are in a French country village, complete with views of a village through a gate. Stroll past the water-fountain statue and the theater marquee, and a toy train may chug past and into the toy store next door.

Turn down the hall to find stone-wall facades and aged wooden and wrought-iron entrances to the stationery, the cigar shop with a magazine rack in front, the wine shop, bank, and grocery. The stone and iron and wood, even the roof tiles, combine in a texture that evokes an aged village, but one that reveals itself like a jewel box of tastes and sensations, one of those earthy places where a person can't help but stop and sample its richness.

This realism comes as no surprise. The owner had Theo Kalomirakis spend a week in Provence studying rural French villages, taking pictures and observing the architecture and its people. And the owner has purchased real elements from the villages, from the cobblestones to the stone walls to the roof tiles and the naturally distressed wooden doors.

Visitors enter through an arched doorway (immediate left) and are instantly transported to a French country village. Even the fan pattern of the cobblestones echoes that from a village in rural France.

There's only one limitation to the palpable images showcased on these pages: this basement-village re-creation doesn't exist—at least not yet. These images are all digital renderings of an entertainment wing in

progress, produced to provide this client of Theo Kalomirakis Theaters with a realistic walk-through of his entertainment space.

The images are produced by Anthony Cortez, who took Kalomirakis's photos from France and combined them with computer models of actual pieces such as the

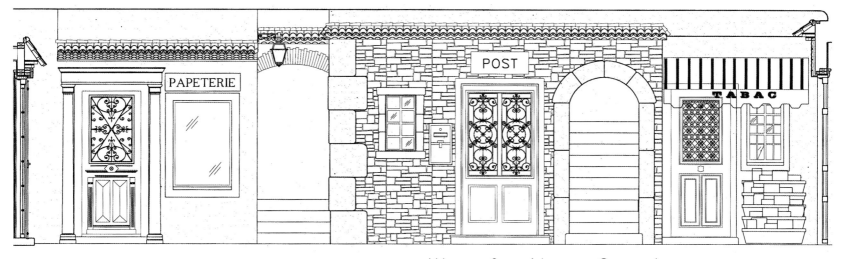

The elaborate details and vaults are modeled after the French Renaissance and baroque theaters of the design firm Rapp & Rapp. The digital rendering includes architectural details that Rapp & Rapp used in many of theaters it built for Paramount in the 1920s.

cobblestones. Some of the images, Cortez explains, consist of more than one hundred separate pieces either texture-mapped or modeled on a computer program.

The stone walls, for example, were texture-mapped from the photos Kalomirakis took, so Cortez did not have to produce each stone separately. The cobblestones, however, were modeled using a process akin to molding a piece of clay on the computer, by moving and adjusting many vertices. Once one cobblestone was produced, Cortez could replicate it, color them differently, and repeat the interesting fan pattern shown in the photos from France.

Realistic lighting is added from sophisticated software programs to create highlights, shadows, and the natural flow of light as it should appear.

The theater was one of the toughest tasks to create digitally, as its ornate ceilings and columns required the mapping and modeling of many elements. Cortez worked from photographs, computer drawings, and paint samples. The column capitals came from catalogue photos, the chairs from photos of Kalomirakis-designed chairs with their beading texture-mapped on top. The template for the ceiling came from computer-aided design (CAD) drawings, and the paintings in the ceiling came from reference books. The bulbs around the ceiling molding detail were modeled, as were the groins where vaults intersect in the corners.

The owner's fun side will be displayed in a toy shop located across from the theater entrance.

At the end of the hallway will be an antiques store and a grocery.
The chalk board lists the day's specials.

The interior of the wine cellar/shop posed additional imaging challenges. The ceiling was mapped from a photo of a log-beamed ceiling in France. The wine racks were modeled in 3-D from the images of the company providing them. The bottles and corkscrew and piece of cheese were also modeled carefully in 3-D. The labels of the old wines were mapped from bottles Cortez purchased. He then spent eight to ten hours of rendering time just to balance the lighting and create the proper reflections off the glasses and the chrome of the corkscrew. He also added layers of dirt and grime to the walls for authenticity.

Next to the wine shop is a cigar shop,
complete with a magazine rack. Even the stone walls from Provence
will be re-created in this authentic great escape.

The rich flavors of Provence come alive even in this digital rendering of the wine shop, which comes from reference photographs collected in France.

In all, Cortez worked about three to four months to prepare this digital image walk-through and an animated version to show the homeowner—and his detailed work is reflected in the near realism of the images. After all, this homeowner doggedly pursued authenticity.

The owner went so far as to purchase the original doors from the Paramount theater in his hometown of Toledo, Ohio, for his own theater of the same name. There was only one problem: the doors were nine feet high, and the ceiling height in this basement space was eight feet. So the ceiling height had to be raised to ten feet to accommodate the doors. Meanwhile, they had been stored in a building in New York, but that building collapsed, and the doors, not found, were presumed to be destroyed. However, they turned up a few months later with an antiques dealer, with whom the owner negotiated their return.

Those doors, like the rest of this authentic French village, will find a home in a certain California basement. We wonder if the wine and cheese served there will taste a little richer.

C R E D I T S

THE KIEV
Senior Designer: Yujin Asai
General Contractor: Roman Shwed
Additional Interior Design: Bill Stubbs
Fabrics: Scalamandré

Audio Video Installation: Robert's Home Audio & Video, Los Angeles, Calif.
Audio Video Installer: Steven Greenen
Audio Video Equipment: Runco, JBL Synthesis, Snell, Faroudja

THE ELLIPSE
Senior Designer: Michael Brothers
General Contractor: Kathryne Sargent
Project Manager: Chuck Loudon
Components Fabricator: J. Frederick Construction, Inc.
Seating: CinemaTech Seating

Audio Video Installation: Marvin Electronics, Forth Worth, Texas
Audio Video Installers: Stewart Schuster, Larry Lawyer
Audio Video Equipment: Runco, McIntosh

THE MOONLIGHT
Senior Designer: Yujin Asai
Associate Designer: Jose Perez
General Contractor: Mike Martin
Additional Interior Design: Jean Ortmier
Poster Artist: Phil Parks
Fabrics: Robert Allen

Audio Video Installation: Genesis Audio & Video, Irvine, Calif.
Audio Video Installer: Darryl Peters
Audio Video Equipment: Runco, Triad, AudioQuest, Lexicon

THE FIRST RUN
Senior Designer: Garry Griggs
General Contractor: Ilex
Project Manager: Delbert Adams
Components Fabricator: Ilex
Seating: Sandringham

Audio Video Installation: Integrated Media Systems, Sterling, Va.
Audio Video Installer: Tom Wells
Audio Video Equipment: Vidikron, JBL, Sony, Pioneer

THE NILE

Senior Designer: Michael Brothers
General Contractor: Chris Mackey
Sculptor/Components Fabricator: Frank Gallagher
Scenic Painter: Doug Bowman
Seating: CinemaTech Seating

Audio Video Installation: Image, Sound & Control, Las Vegas, Nev.
Audio Video Installers: Don Calley, Bill Fischvogt
Audio Video Equipment: Runco, B&K, Triad

THE JEWEL

Senior Designer: Robert Fuller
General Contractor: Bruce Belvin
Fabrics: F. Schumacher
Seating: Acoustic Innovations

Audio Video Installation: Audio Advisors, West Palm Beach, Fla.
Audio Video Installers: Eric Bergstedt, Jeff Miller
Audio Video Equipment: Meridian, Sony, Faroudja

THE TUSCANY

Senior Designer: Michael Brothers
General Contractor: Buzz Rumsey
Acoustical Engineer: Steven Haas
Stage Curtain Mural: Artgroove
Set Fabricator: J. Frederick Construction, Inc.
Seating: Irwin Seating

Audio Video Installation: Atlanta Home Theater, Atlanta, Ga.
Audio Video Installer: Scott Ross
Audio Video Equipment: Digital Projection, Wilson, Meridian, Jeff Rowland

THE DIGITAL PALACE

Senior Designer: David Hutchinson
General Contractor: George Jones
Additional Interior Design: Katherine B. Shields
Seating: Irwin Seating

Audio Video Installation: Electronic Evolutions, Carmel, Ind.
Audio Video Installer: Travis Combs
Audio Video Equipment: Runco, Genelec, Snell & Wilcox, Meridian

THE SOUTH BEACH

Senior Designer: Michael Brothers
General Contractor: Anthony Salcito
Additional Lighting Design: Walter Spitz
Principal Photography: Robert Reck
Set Fabricator: J. Frederick Construction, Inc.

Audio Video Installation: Electronic Design Group, Scottsdale, Ariz.
Audio Video Installers: Tony Tangalos, Chip Satterlund
Audio Video Equipment: Digital Projection, CAT, ADA, Sony

THE LUNADA SUNSET

Senior Designer: Michael Brothers
General Contractor: Carlos Bas
Additional Interior Design: Carl Madsen
Additional Photography: David Kessler
Scenic Painter: Sharon Plum
Fabrics: F. Schumacher
Seating: Irwin Seating

Audio Video Installation: Robert's Home Audio & Video, Los Angeles, Calif.
Audio Video Installer: Brian Dick
Audio Video Equipment: Runco, MartinLogan, Proceed, Marantz, Xplore Solutions

THE TOLEDO

Senior Designer: Aline Rizk
General Contractor: Marc Anderson
Components Fabricator: Formglas
Scenic Painter: Derrick Martens
Seating: Irwin Seating

Audio Video Installation: Aurant
Audio Video Installers: Mike Pyle, Brian Child
Audio Video Equipment: JVC, Proceed, Revel, Sony

THE RITZ

Senior Designer: Aline Rizk
General Contractor: Shafir & Munir
Project Manager: Phil Cuny
Additional Interior Design: Hershel Cannon
Murals: Artgroove
Components Fabricator: Formglass
Seating: CinemaTech Seating

Audio Video Installation: HomeTronics, Dallas, Texas
Audio Video Installers: Greg Margolis, Eddie Asher
Audio Video Equipment: Runco, CAT MBX, ADA, Xplore Solutions

THE SIFNOS

Senior Designer: Yujin Asai
General Contractor: Nicolas Rotas
Wood Fabricator: Ioannis Tzes
Seating: Irwin Seating

Audio Video Installation: Yannis Roumpesis, Ltd., Athens, Greece
Audio Video Installer: Yannis Roumpesis
Audio Video Equipment: JBL, Denon, Philips

THE RIALTO

Senior Designer: Yujin Asai
General Contractor: Vern Buwalda
Interior Design: Lisa Slayman
Seating: Acoustic Innovations

Audio Video Installation: AudioVisions, Lake Forest, Calif.
Audio Video Installers: Mark Hoffenberg, Ted Taylor
Audio Video Equipment: Sony, Lexicon, Triad, Faroudja

THEO KALOMIRAKIS THEATERS
517 W. 35th St.
New York, NY 10001
(877) TKTHEATERS
www.tktheaters.com

Book design and page layout: Jeffrey Rubin, APM ADVERTISING, INC. East Calais, VT, USA, Tel: 800-440-2344

Pre-press: KAPON EDITIONS, Athens, Greece

Procesing of colour images: MICHAILIDES BROS and KAPON EDITIONS

Printer: A. PETROULAKIS S.A.

Binding: G. MOUTSIS

THEATER SECTION ELEVATION

1

1/2" = 1'-0"

4
A-2

[.10m]

DUPLEX OUTLET

PLASTER CEILING PAINTED

FINISHED PLASTER FASCIA

WOOD VENEER PANEL
MEDIUM STAINED FINISH

WOOD VENEER PANEL
MEDIUM STAINED FINISH

WOOD VENEER TRIM
EBONIZED FINISH

LEFT, CENTER & RIGHT
SPEAKERS

ALIGN

CONCEALED
DOUBLE DOORS
TOUCH LATCH
HARDWARE

SCREEN MOUNTED TO
CARPETED WALL